SMALL BUSINESS
Big Heart

SMALL BUSINESS

Big Heart

How One Family Redefined
the Bottom Line

PAUL WESSLUND

Highway 61 Communications, LLC
Louisville, Kentucky

Published in the United States of America by Highway 61 Communications, LLC

Highway 61 Communications, LLC
8101 Barbour Manor Drive
Louisville, Kentucky, 40241

FIRST EDITION

Cover and Interior Design by GKS Creative, Nashville, TN
Cover photo by Christopher Fryer

For special discounts for bulk purchases or to book Paul Wesslund to speak
visit the website at www.paulwesslund.com

Library of Congress Cataloging-in-Publication Data
Library of Congress Control Number 2020904852

Effective Date of Publication August 2020

ISBN: 978-1-7346291-0-1 Paperback (IS)
ISBN: 978-1-7346291-3-2 Paperback (KDP)
Ebook ISBN: 978-1-7346291-2-5 (mobi)
Ebook ISBN: 978-1-7346291-1-8 (ePub)

PRINTED IN THE UNITED STATES OF AMERICA

For Debbie, who believes in me

CONTENTS

CHAPTER 1

They Saw Me
for Who I Could Be

In an odd corner of Louisville, Kentucky, there's a restaurant you'd never find unless you were looking hard for it. The unlikely location hints that this building couldn't have been anyone's first choice for a food-service business. It wasn't. In fact, it could be seen as a monument to second choices—and second chances.

The owners, Sal and Cindy Rubino, made a practice of hiring refugees fleeing conflicts in other countries and people in treatment programs for drug and alcohol addiction. And it paid off.

It paid not because Sal and Cindy set out to do good deeds for people in need, but because they set out to work with people who shared their high standards both for business and for how they lived their personal lives. It paid because Sal and Cindy saw the stories behind the job applicants—instead of seeing a prison record, or someone who didn't speak English, they saw people who had overcome harder tasks than even the daily, competitive grind of a restaurant business. And it paid because Sal and Cindy saw themselves in people who needed a second chance.

Sal and Cindy got so many second chances that it's hard to pinpoint when they finally got on their feet for good. But 2015 offers a place to start a story about a family business that found a way to succeed by living out the same life principles both at work and at home.

By 2015 Sal and Cindy's restaurant had been open in its location for eight years. It had just been featured on the Food Network cable TV show *Southern Fried Road Trip*. Its business practices were about to be recognized by the Louisville Convention and Visitors Bureau with a special Unity Award. It was finally a thriving business.

☙

Trouble finding Sal and Cindy's restaurant in 2015 starts with the name, an achingly generic "The Café." Next comes a forbidding turn off Broadway, one of Louisville's busier streets. It's an easy right turn just two miles from downtown, but it takes you under an old stone railroad bridge into a patchwork of large brick buildings, some in use, some not. One longtime business in the area, the Louisville Stoneware pottery company, might have a tour bus parked out front, or there might just be a couple cars in its tiny parking lot.

Although moving along the curving, curbless streets gives you the feeling of being in a ghost town, if it's lunchtime it's tough to find a parking place. The reason is your destination: a large, blocky building, windowless except for one glass wall looking onto a patio which sits almost directly beneath the trestle that carries several long and noisy freight trains a day.

Outside The Café, knots of people wait for the next table. Inside are more than 100 lunchers—more than 200 on a nice day when the patio's open. About 500 meals will be served until midafternoon, when the crowd thins and many of the tables turn to holding rows of to-go

2

boxes, while the staff preps as many as 500 catering orders for business lunches the next day.

Stepping inside, you first notice the sound—a steady social buzz coming from mostly tables of friends. Business meals at The Café tend to happen over breakfast, when there's less competition from chatter. Under the conversations you hear the background music by XM Radio's "'40s Junction" station—Glenn Miller, Ella Fitzgerald, Frank Sinatra, Nat King Cole. The dining room is large and open, and every kind of antique lamp fixture you can imagine hangs from a black ceiling, lighting the room a warm yellow. The tablecloths are white and covered with glass tops. Under the glass are paper leaves, an art class project from a local elementary school. Gigantic, brightly colored posters of Broadway musicals line the wall opposite the window.

The next thing you see offers a first clue to why the place is so popular. A small round table just inside the door holds three huge cakes: foot-tall cylinders, one easily identifiable by the strawberries sitting on top; next to it a German chocolate cake with a coconut-stuffed frosting; then a black-and-white Tuxedo cake shimmering with a chocolate icing. Each has several chunks carved out of it, a sign that it's smart to order your favorite first, before it's gone—something the regulars have already done.

To the right of the cake table you spot a lectern. In 2015, the host behind the stand is Sal Rubino himself—he hasn't yet found a greeter he's confident can meet his standards for managing the logistics and hospitality of blending customers, tables, and servers. From behind the worn, wooden piece of furniture, Sal looks up, a bald man wearing black-framed reading glasses and a long-sleeved, blue button-down shirt, unremarkable, really, until he looks up at you and his eyes and smile seem to grow and pop out of his face, inviting you in and instantly persuading you that you're in a place you want to be.

"Hey, how are you doing? It's a beautiful day out there. How many do you have today?"

It's a deliberately random line of small talk, carefully thought through like everything else at The Café. "I don't say anything like, 'Is this your first time dining with us?'" says Sal. "Because I might not remember them and they might say, 'Oh, we're regular customers.'"

Sal will likely visit you at your table during your meal. His sunniness is something people cite when you ask why they come to The Café. Some will praise it for hiring refugees and people in recovery, but most don't even know about that—The Café neither hides it nor promotes it. Most mention the cakes as a reason to patronize the restaurant. Many will mention the friendly service, others the large portions—you see a lot of people leaving with containers of leftovers in their hands. But mostly they come for the food.

When you sit down and open the beige three-fold menu, you see four columns listing just about anything you'd want for a meal: a page of soups and salads; a range of sandwiches, all the way across to the children's section, where you find peanut butter and jelly. Flipping the menu over, you see you can have breakfast anytime: traditional eggs, biscuits and gravy, or tributes to Southern traditions like country ham or the Southern Grits Scramble. There are innovative twists like baked oatmeal and a sweet potato cinnamon roll.

Sal does the hiring, runs the dining room, and keeps the books. But the menu is Cindy's creation, crafted over a lifetime of thinking about how to make food that people will like. In the kitchen she works with mostly refugees, from Cuba, from Burma, from Uzbekistan. Each moves around their own workstation, somehow not bumping into each other among the counters, oven, and stove. Cindy's style of greeting a visitor is to ask first about them, how they are, where they just came from. If Sal seems open and welcoming, Cindy comes across as more low-key and personal. Her glasses perch on top of her blonde hair, eyes looking inside you. Those eyes widen and her face animates when you ask about food. She describes The Café's fare as comfort food she strives to make "craveable" by layering flavors. She demonstrates making an omelet with her red onion relish—a blend of Italian red onions, brown sugar, red pepper flakes and soy sauce. She calls it "liquid gold" and a "flavor bomb."

Back at your table you decide on the Country Chicken Salad you've heard people rave about. It doesn't come with fireworks or fol-derol—two scoops of a traditional-looking mayonnaise-based mixture on a bed of leaf lettuce, red apple slices on one side, a small stem of red grapes on the other, and sprinkled with walnuts. Then you taste the flavor layers Cindy talks about—cider vinegar, white pepper, sugar. As you poke into the salad you see the real star of the plate, a mixture dense with tiny cubes of diced white meat, seasoned with parsley, basil, and thyme.

Sal also gives that chicken a starring role when he describes The Café's success. He'll tell you The Café offers "the total package" of good food, low prices, friendly service, and a comfortable atmosphere, each one of those with high standards. But first it's the food.

"We work hard at high quality," he says. "We don't do anything prepackaged. Everything is made from scratch. In our chicken salad we don't use precooked chicken meat like a lot of places. We buy the highest quality, fresh whole chicken breast and roast it in our kitchen."

Sal extends those standards to the quality of the employees.

"We're very selective in who we hire. We work hard at training our staff to provide excellent service, but people have to have a certain natural hospitality. They've got to be able to make eye contact, have a nice smile."

As you finish your chicken salad you might start noticing The Café's differences from other restaurants. It doesn't serve alcohol. It's not open for dinner. It's not open for Sunday brunch. What you probably don't know is that those features resulted from wrenching decisions by Sal and Cindy to keep their family together and to hang on to valued employees. While they sacrificed traditional restaurant profit centers to forge a better work-life balance, they hung on to their five-star standards.

"Don't come in here to apply for a job thinking, 'It's just lunch; how difficult can it be to make chicken salad?'" says Sal. "This is the best chicken salad you're ever going to eat, and the experience we create for our guests is just as high. A lot of time and effort went into making The Café what it is. It didn't just happen."

In 2015, you might have placed your chicken salad order with a server named Melinda Quire. She worked at The Café for only a few months, but Cindy still thinks of her as someone who shows how a life can be changed for the better.

Cindy first saw Melinda at a Christmas party at Priscilla's Place, a transition house for women run by Adult & Teen Challenge of Kentucky, part of a national network of Christian-based centers for drug and alcohol addiction treatment.

Priscilla's Place is a large Victorian house with comfortable living and kitchen areas on the main floor and bedrooms up flights of stairs. The twelve- to fifteen-month residential treatment program allows them to work an outside job after a few months of counseling, Bible study, and classes like anger management. One preferred place for the residents to get a job was The Café, since it was walking distance away and already had experience hiring people in recovery. That relationship between Priscilla's Place and The Café led to an invitation for Cindy to join the board. Cindy agreed. The program resonated with her for supporting its residents in the same way Cindy had felt supported by a church group at a time when she felt like her life was falling apart. "I saw people transformed the way I had been transformed in my heart," she says. "I would witness how they would love on people at Priscilla's Place. I felt very connected to that because it really wasn't so much about addiction as it was understanding how you are loved."

At the 2014 Christmas party at Priscilla's Place, catering donated by The Café, Cindy sat with a group of a half dozen visitors watching an unusual show that's a part of the home's recovery program. A group of the residents gathered, faced the guests, turned on a recording of Christian music, then started accompanying it with sign language hand and arm movements. It's a show they take on the road to area churches.

"It's so expressive, and you can do it without having a singing voice," says Cindy. Among the group of about ten women performing, Cindy noticed Melinda.

"I thought, 'Wow, she's really struggling,'" says Cindy. "She'd been there a week. She didn't know the song yet. She was less animated than the others. I saw it in her eyes. She's like, 'What the heck is going on here? Leave me alone, I can't do this.' She was a broken person. I know we're totally different people. We had totally different experiences, but I connected with her brokenness."

Cindy left the Christmas party and didn't see Melinda again until several months later, as Melinda sat in the dining room with Sal, applying for a job.

Oh wow, this is amazing, Cindy remembers thinking. "Not that she was physically any different, though it looked like she had been taking better care of herself and they'd gotten her some dentist appointments. She wasn't ashamed anymore. She looked as though her heart had been transformed. She had a self-assuredness, an ability to look me in the eye."

❦

Today Melinda remembers that Christmas party in 2014 as a low point in a life of low points. She was thirty-three years old and had arrived from jail after spending nearly half her life dependent on some kind of chemical. For the next several months she would be away from her fourteen-year-old son and five-year-old daughter. They were living back where she grew up, 180 miles north in Indiana. She hadn't seen her son much recently. She was closer with her daughter. But instead of being with them, here she was in Louisville, in a line of women doing sign language to music in front of a group of strangers.

"It was a hard time," she says. "It was the first time I ever missed anything with my kids. I'd never been away from them at all, especially my daughter. She had been with me twenty-four hours a day."

Melinda tells a story of repeated trauma in the matter-of-fact cadence of someone who's told it often in different forms of therapy. She lives in a manufactured house a mile and a half outside a small Indiana town near Muncie, across the county road from her mom and stepdad, rolling grass and farmland as far as you can see, dotted with just a building here and there. She talks in her small living room—round-faced; long, dark hair—wearing a sweatshirt, her eye contact regularly shifting to keep track of her two children. It had been a big weekend. Ten-year-old Salem qualified for State at the regional for her school cheering competition. Draven had celebrated his second birthday at Chuck E. Cheese. A three-foot-tall cage holding three guinea pigs shows off an earlier birthday present for Salem. Cans of Play-Doh sit on the coffee table, and toy cars and trucks are scattered everywhere. Draven occasionally walks over to the grownups in the room to share playtime with a truck, but mostly Salem keeps him entertained in another room as Melinda remembers her first days at Priscilla's Place, five years before.

"When I went there, I lost everything. I lost my family, I lost my house, I lost my car, I lost my kids. Everything I owned I had to have my parents sell to pay them back for what they had given to get me into Priscilla's Place. I told them to just sell anything I had.

"I was missing my kids and wasn't real sure about facing a whole year of staying away from them. I was at the beginning of my journey where I didn't know about all my problems," she says. "I knew I had some problems, but I hadn't dealt with them. I didn't know why I was doing the things I'd done. I still didn't really know how I ended up there and why, for lack of other words, I was such a fuckup. That's how I saw myself then. I was worried about losing my kids for good. I wanted to straighten things up so I could come back and be better for them."

Melinda remembers growing up riding her bike into town, playing down by the river and in the barn, and riding horses. Pets included goats, a peacock, chickens, and a turkey, who "thought he was a dog."

She also remembers being about eight years old when her dad left and her adopted brother committed suicide. A brother she had been close to nearly died in a traffic accident when she was sixteen. A grandfather she had been close to died when she was in her twenties. "I had a lot of abandonment issues going on, rejection issues from school age. Just about every man in my life left in one way or another."

Melinda got a work permit at fifteen and started jobs at restaurants. She hung out at one "party house" in particular, and she spent part of her senior year in high school hiding a pregnancy.

"It was a hard thing to deal with at seventeen," she says. "I had my oldest son a couple months after I graduated high school, so it was very difficult socializing and not feeling accepted. I would go get high and that way I could speak to people I couldn't otherwise."

Melinda says a family history of stomach problems started to affect her, along with other conditions that would lead her to going on disability.

"I have colitis, possible Crohn's, so I was in and out of the hospital a lot and sick," she says. "I had multiple injections for back issues, I have depression and severe anxiety and panic attacks, the whole ball of things."

As a new mom at the time, Melinda says, she was "struggling to keep up at work and to keep our house going." Melinda knew someone in a treatment program that used methadone, a drug used to treat heroin addiction, as a less-harmful substitute that can prevent withdrawal symptoms. Melinda would use part of their methadone dose. "That's when I started using. I wasn't supposed to be getting it and I was using it more to get the high rather than to come off anything."

Melinda was also taking anxiety medication and by the time she was twenty-four she'd had her first overdose. "I was just eating them like candy," she says. After getting her stomach pumped she spent a week in the hospital but soon after started a prescription for stomach pain.

"When things would go wrong I would take more so I could forget about it and keep going," she says. The next few years "were all kind of a blur. I was probably taking between fifteen and twenty pills a day of either Vicodin, Percocet, OxyContins, morphine, Adderalls." She found herself being a caretaker for several other people's children, along with her new daughter. "I was just wanting to get things done. I didn't know how to get out of it. If I quit taking, I knew I wouldn't be able to keep up with all the kids."

As the kids she was taking care of got older, she says, "I hid my addiction from everyone. I was that housewife, I was that mom doing school activities and the classroom parties and sleepovers and nobody knew that I was sneaking off into the bathroom to get high and coming back out and cooking dinner and going to the next event."

But it didn't last forever.

"I lost all my self-esteem, any confidence I had that I could do anything. I had no self-worth. I kept taking more and more because my tolerance was going up and pretty soon it wasn't working for me anymore. It wasn't giving me energy. It wasn't taking my pain away. So I just started taking more of them."

On a family vacation to an amusement park, Melinda overdosed again. She vaguely remembers security guards running toward her, then realizing she was in a hospital rehab unit. She later learned she'd been revived in the ambulance.

"I flatlined," she says. "I've actually flatlined three times; I have physically died three times and they had to bring me back."

Melinda pauses in her story to wonder what it means to come back from the dead.

"Many times I feel like I was meant to do something else," she says. "My son was born a couple years after that, so he would not even exist if I hadn't come back. I still don't know why I got another chance, and what I was meant to do with it. It may just be to take care of my kids. People tell me all the time I have amazing kids."

Melinda left the hospital to return home in order to face charges there for having drug paraphernalia. The judge told Melinda he was going to do her a favor—he would keep her in jail until she could find a place at a drug treatment center. Her parents had been talking with people at Priscilla's Place.

Melinda spent a month in the jail. While there she revived an interest in writing, and on her last day, when she knew she was headed to Priscilla's Place, she wrote what to her is her most meaningful poem.

She wrote it, she says, because "I had my mind set on what I wanted to do when I got there. I had a mission. I was going to change."

The title of the poem is "A New," and it reads, in part:

I'm starting over, this day is anew,
I now know what I have to do.
Hand my life over, pray to my God,
Do my life right, I have to fight.
It won't be easy, no kids here to squeeze me.
Had to go away to learn a new way...
My viewpoint is changing. My thoughts rearranging.
I have faith, I have hope, that I'm done with the dope...
I hand my life over, my lord & savior,
Please help me stay sober.

The new start at Priscilla's Place was a rough start, with anxiety, panic attacks, and claustrophobia. Suddenly without sleeping medication—no drugs were allowed—she struggled. She faced up to a realization about herself.

"Everyone told me that my best and worst quality was the same thing. That I was a giving person. I loved to be able to help people, but at the same time I would give until I had nothing. I would have no money, no food. I wasn't even a good drug addict because I would give my drugs to people and leave myself with nothing. No other drug addict I know would give their stuff to other people. But I did."

Then for the first time in telling this story about addictions and overdoses, Melinda starts crying. Why now?

"I hate to see anybody hurt," she says in a cracking voice. "I hate to see people struggle. I know how it feels. I would rather take that pain on than to see somebody else take it."

So one of Melinda's first requirements at Priscilla's Place was to stop helping people.

"I was not allowed to help people for a week, because they realized it was an issue," she says. "I made myself physically sick trying to help all the girls. I was helping them make their shopping list, and I was doing my stuff on top of it. I would get done and see someone that needed help, so I would go help them clean. I'd only been there a month and I was like the mom of the group. It was way too much."

Another urge to curb was cooking. Melinda discovered she was one of the few women in the house with kitchen experience. She did learn to leave the other cooks alone when it was their turn to fix dinner, but her nights to prepare the meal were popular. A requested dish was the chicken and dumplings she would make while she was growing up. The simple ingredients are chicken, a can of cream of chicken soup, thyme, and canned biscuits for the dumplings. People love it, she says, calling it a cheap and filling meal that's amazing over mashed potatoes.

Melinda learned to set priorities. To let people solve their own problems. She grew more active in the musical sign language performances, even taking the lead role.

Melinda's roommate worked at The Café, and most of Melinda's jobs had been in restaurants, so when Priscilla's Place said she was ready to apply for a job, she walked the half mile to The Café for an appointment with Sal.

"I really liked him from the start," she says. "He was really friendly and outgoing and made you feel comfortable. He's really easy to talk to and we just drifted off into conversation."

Sal says, "She appeared to be someone that was hungry. We needed somebody to wash dishes—that's the only position we had open at the time—and she didn't care. She just wanted a job. I think that's a statement of character."

When Melinda went back to the kitchen, Cindy sensed a hard worker.

"Melinda was pretty tough," says Cindy. "Working a dish machine is very overwhelming, with all those dishes coming at you. And it's a fast, fast pace."

Melinda wasn't fazed by the pace. When she saw a plate of food waiting to be garnished and prepped to be taken to a table, Melinda did it.

"They had someone missing, so I scooted over there to help one day," she says. "The next thing I know, a waitress wasn't there and I said, 'Well, I can take the food out.' So I ended up doing that, too."

Cindy had spent her career watching for workers like Melinda who treated each task as an essential part of the big mission of keeping the restaurant in business.

"You didn't have to tell her, 'Let me show you what else you can do while you're waiting for the dishes,'" says Cindy. "She would just grab on to the next thing. She wouldn't mind going over and washing a pot while waiting for the dish machine to push through. She would just get it done and be back the next day with an attitude of, 'Okay, let's do it again.' She accepted things as they were and realized that she was responsible. She chose a positive response to life."

If restaurant work was second nature to Melinda, there was a culture shock moving from the smallest of Indiana towns to a kitchen staffed by refugees from places around the globe. She didn't figure it out right away.

"I didn't know they were refugees at first; I just thought those were the workers they hired," she says. "There was a definite language barrier, but they were so friendly I wanted to talk to them and hear what brought them there. They had me tasting their hot sauce they brought from their country."

Describing a conversation with one refugee, she says, "She told me how she ended up at The Café and her story about her family and her country and why she came here." Then Melinda says something extraordinary, considering the years of her life she spent in a fog of addiction: "It makes your problems seem real small."

Sitting and talking with a refugee about each others' second chances gave Melinda a new way to look at her new life.

"It's funny because she listened to my problems the same way I listened to hers," she says. "That was the great thing about working at The Café. It's something I never had when I worked at home. At home it was all just people I hid things from. I was friends with them, I went out with them, but I wasn't myself except for the ones I was just getting high with. I never had that sense of family. At The Café they were open to anything. I learned it was okay to share my stuff with other people."

Melinda left The Café after three months. Sal offered her more money to stay, but her mother had just had a stroke, "and I was scared to leave my family. I couldn't bear it if something happened to her."

Melinda marvels at how she's been living—with just herself, Salem, and Draven. It's a much quieter life compared with her years of trying to manage a household of chaotic relationships.

"It's going pretty well," she says in a distracted way, as though she's being cautious about her current good fortune, thinking about the one-day-at-a-time slogan regularly used by Alcoholics Anonymous. "I'm happier than I was."

Melinda regularly visits a counselor. She attended AA meetings until Draven was born and life got too busy to drive the ten miles across the countryside to the nearest session in Muncie. She doesn't really want to go into town anyway. "I know too many people there I don't want to associate with." She doesn't have a regular doctor yet. "I'm scared to go get one. I know I can manipulate them into prescribing drugs. I've done it. I don't want to have that access."

Melinda is still the sort of person too willing to go overboard trying to help people. Controlling that urge is one of her top priorities.

"I've gotten a lot more organized, I watch my time management, I try to schedule things by using the calendar on my phone," she says. "I still catch myself helping the kids and I try to veer away from that. I've learned I can have self-worth through helping people even though I have to find the right balance. I think it's my purpose to help people. I just have to figure out how to do it to a minimum."

Melinda keeps in touch with some of the employees at The Café through Facebook relationships, and on road trips she'll stop there for lunch. She recalls Sal and Cindy attending her graduation from Priscilla's Place, and that "one or the other was always there. They were just really inviting. They didn't look at you like you had all those problems. They looked at what you could be, or what you were becoming. I thought it was weird at the time. I didn't know how to act around them. I thought I had to be different at first until I realized they're not judging me for how I am. I could just be myself even though I was still figuring out who I was.

"I didn't think there were people like that. I thought my family was like that because they were my family. I didn't think there were actually other people that cared. I've never seen somebody with a heart like that."

❧

Just inside the door to the kitchen in The Café there's a whiteboard where Sal will write an inspirational message. One day in blue marker it displayed a quotation from the late celebrity chef Anthony Bourdain:

"In America the professional kitchen is the last refuge of the misfit. It's a place for people with bad pasts to find new family."

Cindy points to a darker message from Bourdain's book *Kitchen Confidential*. That book tells the story of an industry characterized by drug and alcohol overuse, family-killing hours, and abusive work relationships. Sal and Cindy spent a career trying to overcome the excesses of the industry by creating a more humane work environment for their employees and for themselves. In that process they built an innovative management model that did nothing less than achieve financial success by replacing what they thought was wrong with business as usual, with decency and humanity.

Helping them was a long line of Melindas. Here are some of those stories about how Sal and Cindy Rubino created a small business with a big heart.

CHAPTER 2

The Chef and the Marketer Grow Up

The Café's Tomato Dill Soup
Makes 10 servings

1/2 medium yellow or Spanish onion, diced

2 stalks celery, sliced

4 cloves garlic, minced

1/4 cup vegetable or olive oil

1 Tbsp dried dill weed

1 (14.5-oz) can diced tomatoes

1 (14.5-oz) can crushed tomatoes (puree)

1 (46-oz) bottle V-8 juice

1 Tbsp soy sauce

1 Tbsp Worcestershire sauce

1 tsp granulated sugar

Salt to taste

1 Tbsp chicken base (Better Than Bouillon)

1 cup water

1/2 cup heavy whipping cream

Sauté onion, celery, and garlic in 1/4 cup oil with dill weed until tender.

Purée diced tomatoes and sautéed vegetables in food processor.

Add the processed ingredients to the remaining ingredients (except for whipping cream), in a stockpot, and simmer, covered, for 30 minutes.

Whisk cream into soup just before serving. Adjust amount of cream to desired taste and consistency.

C indy Clark stood in the family eat-in kitchen, holding a can of Campbell's tomato soup and thinking about how she could make it taste better. The teenager had just started paying attention to flavors and was about to experiment with a lunch of grilled cheese and soup for herself and Carrie Green, the Clark's long-time housekeeper who came once a week to work alongside Cindy's mom, Jane.

The suburban setting in Louisville, Kentucky, screamed 1974, from the kitchen's avocado appliances to the green, orange, and gold indoor-outdoor carpet. What wasn't visible to the naked eye was the heritage behind the kitchen, from the traditions of Cindy's rural grand-mother, who cooked from scratch, to the more modern practices of her parents, who filled the pantry with the convenience foods of the day.

After a year in the new house, Cindy still hadn't adjusted to the new, fancier neighborhood. She never would. She'd still ride her bike to the old, more working-class neighborhood to see her friends. The distance was less than a mile, but much farther in lifestyle. Her father, George, was blazing trails in another branch of convenience foods. As one of the founding owners of Burger Queen, he had built an empire of nearly 200 fast-food restaurants around the world, riding the wave along with the founding and growth of McDonald's.

In the wake of Burger Queen's success, Cindy's parents started socializing and traveling the globe on business, reporting back on restaurant outings. But when everyone was home, they made a point of sitting together for family dinners. During the week those family meals were get-it-done affairs. On the weekend, more traditional comfort foods like pot roast were on the menu. George cooked the meat; he had been cooking the family meals since his mother died when he was a teen-ager. Jane typically handled the rest of the meal—potatoes, iceberg lettuce with a bottle of Catalina dressing—meals prepared without a lot of steps. Trips to Grandmother's house, on the other hand, meant homemade cooking—scratch tomato sauce, scratch potato soup.

Cindy watched those different approaches to preparing and presenting food, and she still remembers that time in the kitchen with the Campbell's soup as the day she started thinking with a chef's brain. She started thinking that she could create her own cuisine.

Cindy spun the lazy Susan in the closet pantry and pulled out garlic powder to doctor the Campbell's. She added soy sauce and Worcestershire sauce—"flavor amplifiers," she now calls them. They were ingredients that would find their way into her restaurant's Tomato Dill Soup more than twenty years later. But back in 1974, French onion soup was all the rage. So Cindy topped her concoction with a slice of Swiss cheese.

"I asked Carrie, 'How do you like it?' And she said it was good," says Cindy. "I felt like, wow, she likes it. I guess she was my first customer."

❧

Halfway across the country, in Newburgh, New York, Salvatore John Rubino Jr. sat onstage with the other student government candidates for the junior class at Newburgh Free Academy, the town's public school. Sal sensed something wrong. The students were paying less and less attention to the end-of-the-school-year assembly speakers as the background chatter rose. The candidates looked at each other, wondering what to do. The cause of the disconnect from the official presentations seemed obvious but unspoken that day in May 1972. Just the past fall, principal Dr. Leslie Tourville told the local newspaper, "There is more racial tension than there has ever been at this school."

About one year earlier, a dispute at the 2,500-student school over black programming at senior class night had erupted in fights that spilled into the community. Police fired teargas into rock-throwing crowds of people smashing car windshields and breaking into local businesses. The *Newburgh Evening News* reported 26 injuries, including minor gunshot wounds, and 15 arrests. Police cordoned off a section of the city of 26,000.

"It was a scary time," says Alison Taylor today. As a classmate of Sal's—Alison Molloy at the time—she remembers encouraging him to run for junior class president. "He was one of those people my family called the 'rah rahs.' He got people together and cheered them on. He had a big smile and was likable. He had charisma."

Sal decided to get up and speak to the assembly, even though he wasn't sure what he was going to say. Alison remembers, "It was noisy and out of control. But somehow he got people to listen and pay attention. He carried himself well and had a presence about him. He spoke off the cuff about equality and admonished us to back off hating one another."

"No one was in charge," Sal recalls. "No one was getting a hold of things. I'd never spoken in front of a crowd before. I just spoke off the top of my head. I emphasized that we weren't two groups of people. That we needed to come together as classmates to resolve our own issues. That nobody was going to fix it for us. That we were both the problem and the solution."

Sal got a standing ovation and the juniors elected him president. He believes his moment in the high school gym came "from my parents. We're family and we don't argue with one another. We come together. We love one another." The son of an Italian immigrant, Sal says his parents "were always leaders and taught us to be leaders, not followers."

After the election, Sal says, "I remember feeling so empowered, and it forged so many relationships." He recalls working with black students to sponsor school dances. As a senior, Sal was the public address announcer for football games. And when the cheerleading coach wanted to add boys to the squad, she figured others would follow if Sal started, so he agreed to pioneer as a male cheerleader.

When Sal stood up to calm a restless crowd of fellow high school students, he took a risk to bring people together, and it worked. He carried that lesson in leadership through the rest of his life.

❧

Sal's dad, Salvatore, got off the boat onto New York's Ellis Island in 1928, at the age of ten. The boy was coming with his family to join his father, Joseph, who, along with hundreds of thousands of others, had left the chaotic economy of post-WWI southern Italy. After finding a job laying track with the railroad in the Hudson River Valley town of Newburgh, Joseph sent for his family.

Newburgh hugs the Hudson River, an hour from New York City, fifteen miles from the West Point military academy, and an hour from Woodstock and the picturesque Catskill Mountains. Salvatore left Newburgh for the Army Air Corps during WWII, serving four years in England and Germany as a technician, maintaining airplanes. Later, back home in Newburgh, he used the skills he'd learned in the military to open Rubino Refrigeration, an air-conditioning and refrigeration business serving stores and restaurants in the area, as well as the West Point academy and nearby Stewart Air Force Base.

Sal's mom, Maria, was born in Brooklyn, New York, also to southern Italian immigrants looking for a better life in America. Salvatore and Maria met in Newburgh after Maria's family moved there, attracted by the thriving manufacturing and transportation hub on the Hudson River shipping routes. Maria's father, Gerard Colotti, worked at a factory that made candles for the Catholic church, then at another that produced felt to make hats.

Salvatore Jr. took some Italian language courses in high school and college but doesn't remember his Italian heritage being a big part of his growing-up years. Except for the food.

"We had pasta every night," says Sal. "Mom was a good cook. She made spaghetti and meatballs and lasagna. Her mom made raviolis every Sunday. The stuffing for the cheese was ricotta, parsley, and seasonings. She would come over to our house and have this big bowl on the table that she'd use to make the stuffing. She'd roll out the dough on the table with a broomstick, then take a glass upside-down and cut out the raviolis. When she was done, the bowl would still have cheese in it, and I would reach up and lick my fingers.

"We had turkey on Thanksgiving—it wasn't the best meal. My mom didn't know how to cook roast turkey and dressing." Christmas Eve his mom would prepare the traditional Italian Feast of the Seven Fishes, a meal that can include more than seven kinds of seafood. "She'd have octopus three different ways, in tomato sauce and in a salad, stuffed squid, eel, cod. That was something we all looked forward to every year."

The fifth of six Rubino kids, Sal says, "My mom cooked like a freakin' army was coming over. Whatever was left over she put in the refrigerator and you would eat on that through the week. Always Italian."

Sometimes it seemed there really was an army to feed.

"The family dinner wasn't really a special occasion; it was part of our life," says Sal. "My two older brothers would go back and forth making up creative stories. They probably could have written for a sitcom. My friends came to these dinners. Our house was like Grand Central Station. We didn't have parties, but our home was always open for us to bring our friends over."

One of those everyday dinners especially sticks in Sal's memory, when he invited two of his school friends from the wealthier side of town to the Rubinos' more modest neighborhood.

"I remember them being enthralled with the experience, talking, and storytelling; it was this bustling dinner table. A cacaphony of stories. They left saying they loved the food. My mom cooked pasta, eggplant parmesan, made meatballs from scratch, lasagna, manicotti. I remember vividly how my friends told me what a great time they had. How it wasn't like that at their house."

❧

Salvatore Sr. was a proud man. A proud Italian-American, with the emphasis on the American. He would tell his namesake son how as a kid he would carry around a little American flag.

He was a proud business owner. When Sal Jr. reached high school he went to work for his dad, just like his other brothers, helping install and service air-conditioning systems and walk-in refrigerators. He remembers riding in the truck with his father through the towns along the winding roads of the Hudson Valley. His father would point to restaurants and stores and say, "I piped that job. I piped that job."

And Sal's dad wanted to pass along to his son that work should be done with decency and fairness—on a repair call, you don't just put more freon into a refrigeration system without checking for a leak.

"In the little spare time that he had, he made it a point to interact with me and show me that I was important to him," says Sal, even if the interaction was awkwardly pointing to the 1970s hairstyle that covered his ears. "He would say things sarcastically, like teasing me about my long hair, 'Oh that's a cute little girl.' But the overall impression I distill everything down to is his honesty and that he was a man of character."

"He would ask me questions about my life and what's going on, and it would always get around to doing the right thing and honesty. He wanted me to understand how important it was not to cheat," says Sal. "He liked to show his competitive point of difference. That when you do business with Sal Rubino, you get what you pay for. You don't get taken advantage of. He was sharing that with me as a life tool."

Over the years, Sal Sr. cut back on the pressures of small-business ownership. He dropped employees. He moved out of ownership and into working as a salesman for a larger company. He taught sales courses at the local community college. He got elected to several terms as president of the local country club and developed into an excellent golfer, winning hole-in-one awards.

For some of the golf tournaments, Sal would caddy for his dad. He says, "His colleagues would pull me over and say, 'You know, your dad is not like the rest of us. We're all cussing, carrying on about women and stuff, and your dad would never participate in that.' Everyone looked up to my dad as a person of integrity."

But Sal also saw a father who worked too hard for too little money. He remembers his father making a point of fixing breakfast as a way to spend time with the family, but who otherwise came home, read the paper, and went to bed. He developed ulcers at an early age. And young Sal thought labor was at the wrong end of the job market.

"My dad owned his own business, but he handled his own repairs, so most of the time he wore coveralls and his hands were covered in grease. He looked like a mechanic, and I didn't want to be a mechanic," says Sal. "His customers were dressed nice and had these palatial homes. We lived in a little Cape Cod that didn't have any air conditioning."

Sal also liked things, and he figured out early you need money to buy things. As a boy it was candy; in high school it was record albums. So Sal was open to the lessons in entrepreneurship and leadership he learned from his mom, who was active in the PTA and who kept the books for Rubino Refrigeration, and from helping both of his parents at the Catholic church bingo parlor.

"I was the concession boy," he recalls. "My mom ran the kitchen, so she prepared all the food that was like dinner, and my dad called the numbers onstage. I pushed a little cart that had Cokes and candy bars, and I would sell them and they would give me tips. At the end of the night I might make five or ten dollars. I saw how my parents were running the show and all the other parents were sitting, playing bingo, and smoking cigarettes."

At ten years old, Sal inherited his brother's 150-customer route delivering the local newspaper. But Sal had a different way of delivering papers.

"I had a group of little kids that would follow me around, and I would give them three or four newspapers and I'd point to this building and say, 'A, B, C, and G,' and they would lay papers in front of those doors. I would give them a little bit of money. That was my introduction to human resources and market economy and business management. I learned nothing comes to you. You have to go get it.

I learned how to collect money from people. I know several grown adults that can't look somebody in the eye and say, 'You owe me money; would you please pay me?' I learned that's OK. It's nothing rude. It's just business."

Sal's next venture into entrepreneurship started at a roller rink the summer after eighth grade, when a group of friends introduced him to smoking marijuana. "I said to myself, I could either buy this stuff from money that I make from another job or I could buy enough to sell off and get my share for free."

Sal would smoke and sell pot for the next few years. A wannabe hippie, he'd smoke pot in his bedroom, convinced his mom's Italian cooking would cover up the aroma. He would bicycle or hitchhike into the mountains for hiking and swimming, once discovering a remote café with live music. The day his junior year ended, he walked directly out of the school building, stuck out his thumb, and hitchhiked to join a friend on artsy Cape Cod, Massachusetts. His friend got him a summer job on a fifty-foot schooner, taking tourists out for day cruises. Sal earned $50 a week with free lodging, living on the sailboat.

In his senior year, Sal figured he needed to start getting more serious about what he would do with his life. He looked at elective courses he could take. He enjoyed a ceramics class that got interrupted by a thirteen-day teachers' strike that fall. He received the school's poet of the year award. He got interested in ocean explorer Jacques Cousteau, and he liked *National Geographic* magazine, so he thought he might pursue nature photography. In a photography class, he earned an *A*. He got a job in the camera department at one of the then-popular catalog showroom stores. Sal loved that. Not only did he work with photography, but the department was next to the record and stereo section, feeding his passion for music. But after the Christmas rush, Sal got laid off.

"I had a zeal for making money," says Sal. He ramped up his marijuana business, making a deal to sell some pills. "That's what got me into trouble. I don't even know what they were."

One February night Sal met a friend outside a restaurant to make a handoff, but instead his friend ran toward waiting police. Other cars pulled up; officers drew guns and approached Sal. He was taken to the station and strip-searched. His parents hired a lawyer, and the case was dismissed over questions about whether the police followed proper procedures, and because of Sal's cooperation with the investigation. "It scared the crap out of me. I just decided I wanted to get out of Newburgh."

Sal knew he could go live with his brother Joe, who was teaching high school in Miami. He had to wait—graduation was still more than three months away. But as soon as the ceremony ended, Sal went directly to the airport and got on a plane to Florida, where he would find a career, meet his wife, and eventually move with her to a new life in Louisville, Kentucky.

ɔ

Before Cindy Clark was born, her father lived his own version of the iconic movie moment from 1967's *The Graduate*—the heavily satirical scene showing the new and overwhelmed college graduate played by Dustin Hoffman listening to career advice from a family friend: "I want to say one word to you. Just one word…Are you listening?… Plastics…There's a great future in plastics."

For George Clark, about ten years earlier, the word was *demographics*—the study of population groups. He embraced the advice, and it made him a very wealthy man. George's life zig-zagged toward that demographics moment, along the way picking up the traits he would need to be able to turn that advice into a business.

His influences came from different worlds. He grew up in rural Meade County, Kentucky, with family in nearby Louisville. His parents farmed and his dad was a licensed plumber and electrician. Louisville lay less than sixty miles away, but that didn't measure the cultural distance.

George hated the boxes of hand-me-down clothes he would get from his city cousins. He wanted to wear overalls like his friends. His mom would get mad on the weekend trips to visit the family.

"When we would go to Louisville to be with the family, they would say to the kids, 'Show your family what you've learned,'" George remembers. "The city families always had something new, whether it was some kind of fancy new dance step, or spelling *hippopotamus* backward. Then they would say, 'Hey, George, you do something,' and I would say, 'We had two new calves last year, and one of them we're going to use for beef,' and they'd all laugh. It really pissed my mother off that they were putting us down."

But George loved the cardboard boxes of books from the cousins.

"I had books at the haystack. I had books in the corncrib. I had books by my bed."

When he was in eighth grade, he saw soldiers returning from WWII starting a local baseball league. George wanted in, so he told his father he needed a glove.

"My dad says, 'You don't need a ball glove,'" George recalls, reciting an instruction for life he'd heard from his father before, and would hear again. "You're either reading or working."

જી

George's earliest memories showed him the power of a river to create, and then to end, a community. He grew up along the Ohio River on Kentucky's northwest border, where the closest town was a short boat ride across the river to tiny New Amsterdam, Indiana. When he was three he remembers his mother, Edith, holding him up to look out the window at the boats of people out for a cruise, turning around to head back to Louisville. He remembers that as his mother hoisted him, he burned his arm on the globe of a kerosene lamp—electricity had not yet come to the remote parts of Kentucky.

When his mother needed groceries, he would head to the river, narrow enough there to have a conversation with someone on the other side. Captain Greer would row him to the general store in New Amsterdam, where they'd fawn over him. "'Captain Greer, bring that boy in here,' and I could smell the cookies as soon as I got in the door. 'Reach in there and get yourself a cookie. You're the best damn man that's been in here for weeks.' I loved to go to the store. There was no life vest, just an old man rowing the boat, and an hour later we'd be back with the groceries."

The river took that life away when George turned four. The historic 1937 flood washed their house away and they moved farther inland to live with George's great-grandfather on his farm in the nearby town of Rhodelia.

George's father, George Clement Clark, more familiarly Clemmie or G.C., worked maintenance at a quarry. But he put his plumbing and electrician license to another use—few people in Meade County had indoor plumbing, and Clemmie could install a simple bathroom.

George remembers his first job as a four- or five-year-old, helping his dad install a bathroom for the owner of the Farmers Deposit Bank in the county seat of Brandenburg.

"My job was to hand my dad the right black or white tile for the patterned floor. I loved it. I felt like I was really doing something, and the banker came by and would brag on me." In telling that story, George pauses, gives the wry smile of someone tattling on himself, and says, "I think that's why I have the ego I do." George would move up to handing his dad the right wrench, learning the difference between a 3/8 and a 5/8 open end.

One rainy Sunday morning on the way back from church, driving up the dirt road to their house, the car radio announced that Pearl Harbor had been attacked. George's mother asked her husband if he thought he would have to go. No, said Clemmie, not with a farm, four kids, and a trade. He never did receive a draft notice.

During those years Clemmie would tell George on a Sunday afternoon to bridle up the horse for a visit with the neighbors. Clemmie read the local newspaper and knew the federal government's Rural Electrification Administration and the local electric cooperative were organizing to finally bring in electricity.

"My dad said, 'If we don't have enough people signed up to participate in this, there'll never be a light pole between Brandenburg and Rhodelia,'" says George. "They would tell him no: 'I've heard other people tell about that damn electricity—your chickens quit laying eggs; your bull goes sterile.'"

But Clemmie didn't take "no" for an answer. Decades later, George got called out of a meeting in his Burger Queen executive offices. It was the Meade County Rural Electric Cooperative on the phone, asking what to do with the seventeen $15 payments Clemmie had made to sign the neighbors up as co-op members back in the 1930s that had been earning interest ever since. George and the co-op agreed to donate the money to a local athletic center.

Boys growing up in rural Meade County in the 1940s expected their careers would be full-time farming—no need to finish high school. George's parents had different ideas. During the war years Clemmie would say, "We're living in an environment of illiterate people, and you're going to be the one that understands and reads and knows what the world is about. You're going to pick up the newspaper, you're going to have some chores you do, then you're going to have maybe an hour before I get home. And after we eat tonight, we're going to take the paper, and it's going to have a map of the war in it. It's going to show the line and the bad guys are here and the good guys are here. You're going to know that. I'm going to sit in my easy chair here and we're going to talk about it."

George thought enough of himself to figure that his worldly knowledge from all that reading entitled him to run for class president as a freshman at Meade County High School in Brandenburg, population 800, twenty miles away. He got elected. And again the next year. He played for the baseball and basketball teams. He raised cattle as part of the Future Farmers of America. He benefitted from his dad's plan to buy a school bus that the school board would operate. George started by driving the bus up the road to pick up the driver. By the time George was a senior, he was driving the whole way, picking up students while the adult driver sat behind, drinking coffee or eating a sandwich.

"The last half of my senior year, he wasn't sitting there anymore. He had a heart attack and died," says George. "You haven't seen power until you've seen a teenage boy with a busload of kids. You open the door, *shuu-shuuu*, and two girls get on. Can you imagine what this does to your ego? *Shuu-shuuu*."

Even with all that attention, George was biding his time, figuring he would get through his classwork, learning what he calls "agricultural arithmetic," just enough to graduate, then become a farmer.

"I went through grade school more interested in, did I get four pigs, did I get eight pigs, and what's that going to be worth a year from now?"

Then when George was a week from the end of his junior year in high school, his mother died after falling against a beam while working in the barn, weighing hay for sale. With four younger siblings, an older sister who had married and moved away, and a father working an out-of-town job, George knew he needed to step up. He taught himself to cook for the family, and reassured them, telling them, "We're going to get through this."

"It changed me from being a smart-aleck kid."

George turned to a summer job helping at the Mathieson Chemical plant in Brandenburg and went back there in 1952 after graduating high school—until October 19, when a steel tank exploded, killing one man and injuring several others. George left a Louisville hospital with a damaged eardrum, something he figured would surely keep him out of the military, as he got ready to respond to his draft notice.

But halfway around the world, thousands of American soldiers were dying every month in Korea after nearly two and a half years of war. George drove forty-five miles to the nearest recruiting center in Elizabethtown, Kentucky, climbed the stairs, and saw a sergeant for the newly formed US Air Force leaning against a doorframe, watching for someone to fill his quota.

George tested poorly. Except for "off the charts" mechanical and electrical aptitude. "You knew every damn tool we asked you about."

The Air Force said they'd send George to school, so he signed up for eight years, with the promise of learning aviation electronics. George trained at Lackland Air Force Base near San Antonio, Texas, then was assigned to Knoxville, Tennessee.

The Korean War ended in July of 1953, resulting in budget cuts and layoffs. The Cold War was just beginning, splitting the world over the fear of nuclear war between the Soviet Union and the United States. The US military maneuvered to adjust. The Air Force, as a separate branch of the military, was only six years old, and bureaucratic infighting at the Pentagon raged as the Army, Navy, and Air Force carved out their roles. The infighting came to George in the form of a visit from a colonel forming a unit of the Air National Guard in Louisville. George could finish his military commitment as a civilian employee of the Air Guard, and at night he could take classes at the local Bellarmine College.

George flunked his Bellarmine entrance exam, and that's when he met demographics. A teacher coached him to pass the test the second time, and suggested he study what would later be called the baby boom. He told George about the explosion of births since the end of WWII, and how there were 80 million kids who would need to go to school and be fed. "I know what's coming," he told George. "And those who listen and pay attention are going to reap great rewards."

"I believed all that," says George. He studied hard, earning the ridicule of friends who partied on the weekends while George studied. He foresaw 80 million three-year-olds telling their parents they wanted a Coca-Cola. Of course they'd want fries with that. He picked up a brochure about a new kind of restaurant named McDonald's and decided to write a paper on it.

While George was going to night school, he trained pilots on flight simulators for his military civil service job in the Air Guard. One weekend, a pilot named Jim Gannon, nickname of Mic, walked in. George describes him as a pilot who had what Tom Wolfe describes in his book about test pilots and astronauts as "the right stuff"—the cool, commanding presence that can calm a crisis. Mic grew up working in an eight-stool restaurant in Minneapolis, and he told George he'd like to be in the restaurant business. George had just gotten off the phone with McDonald's, researching his paper. He preached the gospel of demographics to Mic. Mic was an eager convert.

The pair teamed up, squeezing entrepreneurial work into their schedules with the Air Guard. George brought his demographics knowledge and fast-food research; Mic brought a pilot's courage and swagger. Applying for startup loans in the mid-1950s was not easy. "We got kicked out of every bank in Louisville, as we should have. Two broke guys, no experience." They talked to everyone they knew, leading them to Harold and Helen Kite, who were riding the McDonald's fast-food wave with a small chain of Burger Queen restaurants based in Winter Haven, Florida. That's where George and Mic started noticing similarities between the development of fast food and another growing baby-boom business: convenience stores. Both needed a lot of the same things—a patch of land for a building and parking, and an up-and-coming suburban neighborhood. They switched from meeting with banks to meeting with real estate developers, where they found a warmer reception.

George and Mic scrambled to chart their futures in a military adapting to new global defense strategies, and to balance that with their personal ambitions. They finally got a bank loan and bought the franchise rights to open a Burger Queen. George married Jane Shaklette, who he'd met in high school, and they had a daughter they named Cindy. By the time George left the Air Guard in 1962, construction had started on the Burger Queen in Middletown, 14 miles southeast of downtown Louisville.

A year later they opened a second Burger Queen south of Louisville. Moving quickly, they opened a third in the town of Shelbyville, 30 miles east of Louisville.

George was still hungry to learn. He paid attention to customers and listened. When he noticed a regular customer eating outside on a bench, he expanded on the fast-food tradition of drive-ins and walkup windows by adding a dining room. He focused on efficiency, and now, at 86 years old, he still notices how servers at McDonald's use their pivot foot in turning to serve him a cup of coffee. Cindy remembers George taking the family to Louisville's first McDonald's. "He would get out of the car and we would sit there and eat our food and he would go look in the window at their cooking line to see how they did it so he would know how to set up his Burger Queen." George told one interviewer, "If I had looked at McDonald's and had seen someone turning hamburgers while he was hanging from his feet, I would have copied it."

George formed a friendship with the local McDonald's bread supplier. He read industry trade magazines. By 1974, the Florida-based operations had expanded to 10 Burger Queen locations. George's Kentucky-based franchises grew to 55. He became president and chief executive officer of a chain that grew to 180 restaurants in five states and four foreign countries. He moved to a penthouse in a trendy Louisville condo, complete with jacuzzi and marble bathtub. When he was starting Burger Queen, he had a pilot's license and a small plane. As the company grew, he would become a passenger on a corporate jet with its own pilot.

"He lived a very big life," says daughter Cindy. "He had custom shoes. People would come to our house to measure him for suits. It was a very showy life. He hung with the movers and shakers."

That big life was a long way from Cindy's early years when George was out during the week in flight simulator school in Illinois and Jane worked the night shift as a nurse. In those days, Cindy spent a lot of time with her mom's mom, Mary Alice. They all called her Mamaw.

"Cindy loved her Mamaw," says George. "She would work on Cindy's hair, then she'd say, 'Let's go fix supper.' She was known to be the best cook in Meade County."

"She just loved feeding people," Cindy remembers. "She was always talking about recipes as part of her Meade County homemakers group. They would get together and bring in a dish and would try new things, and they even published their own little cookbooks. I still have those little cookbooks."

Cindy struggled through school as the family moved through new neighborhoods, incomes, and social statuses. Her first job was, of course, working at a Burger Queen, earning money to buy a car. She grew up between two worlds. Unlike her much younger sister and brother, she wasn't used to parents on the cocktail party circuit and flying around the world on business trips.

Cindy knew her high school grades wouldn't get her into a top college. She figured she'd spend two years at the local Jefferson Community College, in hopes of improving her prospects. And things did start looking up. She liked the smaller class sizes, the less-regimented schedule, and the absence of social cliques. "You didn't have to fit into a category. It was mainly low-income adults going back to pursue another career. It wasn't about this group or that group. It was just people going to class. I didn't have to pretend to be anybody."

Cindy's appreciation for that kind of egalitarian community would grow over the years into a way of managing employees at her own restaurant.

At community college in the mid-1970s, Cindy still wasn't connecting with the accounting and marketing coursework, but it was different with their culinary program.

"I liked learning how to cook for a large group, using this big equipment, big kettles. I took French in high school and I liked learning how to use the culinary French terms."

During college Cindy worked at the New Orleans House, an upscale seafood restaurant that attracted a lot of downtown Louisville convention business. She ran the buffet, and she would regularly walk among the tables passing out appetizers, earning the nickname "the frog-leg girl."

Cindy also saw the difference between the professional image projected in the dining room and the grittier reality of the people who ran the kitchen.

"It was two different societies. The kitchen was run by sketchy, rough kids. It takes a hard kind of person to do that kind of work. You can't be sensitive to smells or handling raw things or cleaning the guts out of something. They didn't cut me any slack. All the food was in the basement of this old building and you had to go down there by yourself. It was dark and you just didn't want to be alone with any of them. It's like the rough kids on the playground; they're going to set you up to fail. They probably thought I was a spoiled little rich girl, but I didn't want to be the one to quit. It probably had something to do with proving something to my parents—that I was cut out for the hard stuff, that I could stand my ground."

As Cindy's graduation approached it was time to figure out how to combine her experience and schooling into a clearer career path. Her dad helped. He called on a consultant from his contacts with the National Restaurant Association, who recommended culinary schools, including a new one starting up at Florida International University in Miami. Cindy applied and got accepted—fortunately, because she didn't apply anywhere else—and enrolled for the fall semester.

And Cindy helped herself. At Jefferson Community College, she had run across a signup sheet for a summer job: *How would you like to work for a food service at a national park?* That sounds awesome, she thought. Her dad's consultant agreed to be a reference for an application to Yellowstone National Park.

With a junior college diploma, Cindy headed to the airport for a summer in Wyoming, then culinary school in Miami, and a life in an industry she was only beginning to understand.

CHAPTER 3

Romance and Restaurant School

Whiffenpoof Snapper Caprice
Recipe makes one serving.
Increase as needed to make number of servings desired.

6- to 8-oz red snapper fillet

1 banana

Paprika

Salt

2 Tbsp butter, melted

2 tsp fresh-squeezed lemon juice

Spray the pan lightly with nonstick spray. Put fish fillets (6- to 8- ounce fillets per portion) in pan.

Thinly slice bananas lengthwise and place the long slices on fish.

Sprinkle with paprika and salt to taste.

Pour melted butter (2 Tbsp. per fillet) and fresh-squeezed lemon juice (2 tsp. per fillet) over fish.

Broil 5 minutes, until banana edges are brown.

Then bake 10 minutes at 350 degrees.

J ust a few hours after graduating from high school in New York, Sal Rubino stepped off a plane in Miami without much of a plan other than that he could stay with his brother Joe. Joe helped Sal open a checking account—he'd had a bank account, but never a checking account. Sal bought a 1963 Ford Fairlane for $250, teaching himself to replace the ripped fender with one from a junkyard. He drove the car for several years until the engine burned up. Sal didn't know you were supposed to put oil in it.

He enrolled in Miami-Dade Junior College. With his high school photography class and his department store experience selling cameras, he figured he'd pursue a career as a nature photographer. He still hoped to take pictures for Jacques Cousteau, so he signed up for classes in photography, marine biology, and scuba diving. He got a job asking tourists at the Miami hotels if they wanted their picture taken.

When Sal's money started running low his brother suggested he work at a restaurant, and he knew a place. Just down the street was a 25-table Italian eatery named Michelangelo's. It seemed a natural fit for Sal, since he grew up in a house where Italian was cooking in the kitchen every day. He walked down the street to apply, but the owner exploded with laughter at the idea of someone with Sal's 1974-style beard and long hair working at his restaurant.

Sal slunk out to get his hair cut. He went home and shaved. He went back to Michelangelo's and told the owner, "My name is Salvatore Rubino and I'd like to work here." They hired him on the spot as a busboy.

Sal did whatever they asked and in two months he was waiting tables, giving him the income he needed. Sal saw significance in his boss's name—Sal—and his wife's name, Theresa. "To me it was like divine providence that I should work with somebody that has my name and his wife's name is the same as my sister's. I became his protégé and eventually came to be the equivalent of a dining room manager."

One of the regulars was the photographer for the Miami Dolphins. Sal tried to cultivate him as a professional contact. "He never really picked up on my hints."

Sal graduated from junior college with an associate's degree in fine arts and photography. But restaurants paid the bills. Sal branched out beyond Michelangelo's. He got another job at a fancier white-tablecloth continental restaurant. That's where he heard about a unique downtown restaurant, Food Among the Flowers, run by a florist who set the dining room up as a brick patio full of trees and planters, with fresh flowers on the raw wood tables. Sal got a job and worked there for about a year. Today he remembers the decor and the use of antiques at Food Among the Flowers as one of the influences for The Café, and as the site of one of the first lunch dates with his future wife.

But it was the Whiffenpoof in Coral Gables, southwest of downtown Miami, that planted the seed that would grow into a career. The Whiffenpoof evoked New Orleans, with loads of red velvet. Sal did some work in their kitchen, where he met his first French chef.

"He was very creative. He was the first one that inspired me to want to learn how to cook," says Sal. "He had this one dish—he called it Snapper Caprice—which was filet of red snapper that he covered with sliced bananas. It was a signature dish and it was just the oddest combination of things, but it was just delicious. I thought it was something I could learn how to do. It was simple and I would cook it for guests."

Sal's next step toward a life in restaurants came when Michelangelo's owners invited him for a cruise along Miami's intracoastal waterway.

"I remember thinking, wow, they have a nice house, a big boat, they own their own restaurant. That's really cool. I was motivated by money a lot when I was younger and I thought, that's a career to reach my financial lifestyle. My wheels started turning and I'm thinking, I could do this. I could own my own restaurant."

So when Sal started meeting co-workers who were students at the School of Hotel, Food, and Travel Services at the relatively new Florida International University in Miami, Sal enrolled. "I realized you could get a degree in restaurant management."

His most consequential course turned out to be Meat Science, once a week from 8:00 a.m. to noon in a big lecture hall. A lot of the students had been up working in a restaurant until late the night before, and now they sat in a darkened room, looking down at a screen flashing pictures of cuts of meat, as the professor droned in a deep Boston accent about the anatomy of beef, pork, chicken, lamb, goat, shellfish. The only relief was the professor cracking occasional jokes about animal parts—jokes lost on a lot of the sleeping students. Sal thought they were funny, and he heard one other student laughing. He waited after class to meet the woman who shared his sense of humor.

ℰℐ

Cindy Clark loved her summer of 1978 at Yellowstone National Park. She met students on their summer jobs from all over the world. They did a lot of hiking and hard work. Their restaurant near the Old Faithful geyser was the biggest and busiest in the park, and she learned techniques from cooks from across the region. A lot of the cooking was institutional—opening bags of prepared food and dumping them into steamers. But breakfast was cooked to order.

Learning to cook breakfast fast and for crowds would serve Cindy well decades later when her own restaurant had to quickly create a morning menu. One of the cooks taught Cindy how to flip an egg to order in the pan. You start with toast. When you can flip a piece of bread with a wrist-flip of the pan, you move to actual eggs. Lots of broken yolks later, she mastered the technique of when to flip for over easy, over medium, over hard. And she learned the essential kitchen art of what today we would call multitasking.

"You've got six pans, these are over easy, these are over medium, these are scrambled, you got these going at the same time, you learn to keep lots of things in your head at once. Full service has different courses and it's got to be timed to the steak in the oven and that has to be timed to the rest of the table of customers. You've got to know when to start your item based on how long it has to be in the oven. The expediter (that's the worker who takes the plate from the cook, puts on the final items, and hands it to the waiter) is calling out this dish and it's going with this dish so you're listening to all the cues of who needs what so you can put a whole table together."

Up until then, Cindy's experience had been mostly with fast food at Burger Queen. Yellowstone "was one of the first places where I got a taste of large food production where you had multiple components going at the same time."

Cindy found herself fitting in to each new world she entered since the awkwardness of high school and her struggles with business classes. From the big kitchen equipment and collegiality of community college to the busyness of her Yellowstone summer, she would take an even bigger step into the food industry by starting her four-year degree at Florida International University. Its Hospitality Management program was just a few years old and it was hiring teachers out of restaurants, bringing their practical experience into the classroom. "They weren't your typical professors who have been teaching a long time. They were industry leaders who now found themselves teaching. It seemed like more real-life experience.

"It was the perfect fit," says Cindy. "I loved Florida. We'd go on family vacations to Florida, and I liked the idea of going somewhere where I didn't know anyone. Kind of a fresh start."

Cindy took the food courses—foundations of cooking, the history of modern cuisine, sauces—but as much as she liked what she was learning, her career path was still a work in progress. She imagined herself working at an upscale hotel, because that's where fine dining was in those days. The notion of a celebrity chef was pretty much Julia Child's show, *The French Chef*, which had premiered on public television in 1963. Cable TV's Food Network wouldn't go live until 1993. Cindy's path forward was not clear.

"There weren't a whole lot of boutique restaurants. And there weren't very many women in my classes," Cindy recalls. "It was male-driven, and we weren't taken seriously. There were few places for women in the kitchen—either cold food or pastry."

❧

In the Meat Sciences class, Cindy also noticed one other person laughing at the professor's dry wit. She and Sal chatted after class and Sal offered to take her sailing for a first date. Sal had worked on a sailboat one summer and this would be a chance to show off.

But there were no single-hulled boats available to rent that day, so Sal decided to try a catamaran—a boat that's essentially two pontoons connected by a short seating platform with the mast in the middle. The boat immediately flipped, and Cindy treaded water for an hour while Sal tried to right the unfamiliar craft, until he finally flagged down another boater to help him flip it upright.

Future dates tended toward dining out, when they weren't working at a restaurant themselves. They'd explore the city's diverse cuisine, especially the Cuban and other Latin influences. Cindy got jobs at a Holiday Inn, a small Italian restaurant, and an upscale vegetarian restaurant—a unique concept in the mid-'70s. She tried her hand at the more lucrative serving jobs where income gets supplemented with tips, "But I didn't feel like I belonged in the front of the house. I was very shy."

Cindy's expertise and comfort in the kitchen and Sal's more outgoing marketing and networking personality formed the basis for a professional partnership that would characterize the rest of the couple's career.

Cindy and Sal both vividly remember their eyes being opened by a hospitality management course taught by Mike Hurst, a founding faculty member of the culinary school, and a dynamic owner of two large and successful restaurants in Fort Lauderdale.

"Marketing was huge for this man," says Cindy. "He broke down the dining experience into very small components and viewed it as entertainment. I had never really understood that dining could be entertainment. We were on the very cutting edge of when the restaurant business exploded in the '70s, when dining out became more than just a meal. It was about making it more of an experience, and he knew it was going to be big. These theme restaurants were just opening up. TGI Fridays had one of the first packages where you were trained, and it was very intense to work there. Waiters were bringing home tons of money, $200 a night, back in the '70s."

"He had a big personality" is how Sal remembers Hurst's class. "He talked about hiring. He said, 'Some of my best employees are part-time. The single mom who is trying to raise a couple of kids and she's on her own, but she has a great personality, she can laugh at herself, she can make other people laugh.' He talked about how he would do events. If a circus came to town, he would approach them and ask them to bring some animals and parade them through the restaurant. He taught us about value of making guests feel welcome and appreciated, and creating an experience, that wow factor. You want people to come and say, 'this is great; we want to come back.'"

High standards for hospitality and valuing the personality of employees would come to be guiding forces for Sal and Cindy.

ᗉᕽᓇ

Like a lot of students at a culinary college, Sal and Cindy would talk about opening their own restaurant. It would be a casual café with a warm, European feel. They both liked antiques, the chairs and tables wouldn't match, the food would be comfortable, approachable, not pretentious. Cindy would be the chef and Sal would work the front of the house. The name would be Scarborough Fair, which was the title of a Middle Ages ballad about a series of impossible tasks, as well as the name of an annual market in the English town of Scarborough. And of course there was the Simon and Garfunkel song that updated the ballad.

"Cindy's emphasis was culinary; my emphasis was marketing," says Sal. "So I thought we could do a radio jingle—'Are you going to Scarborough Fair?'"

Sal and Cindy saw the ballad's traditional lyrics in a book of English folk songs, illustrated with line drawings of a carousel. The image of a carousel horse would serve as the logo for the restaurant they would open fifteen years later.

ᗉᕽᓇ

Graduation was approaching, and Sal and Cindy decided Miami in 1980 was not the place to stay. In 1979, a broad-daylight shootout launched years of violence in the area as the Medellin drug cartel consolidated and grew its business. In May of 1980, riots broke out after four Dade County Public Safety Department officers were acquitted in the death of a black salesman and former marine.

"Miami was a crazy place in the early '80s," says Cindy. "We'd had enough. We decided we'd go be ski bums for the winter."

Cindy had been on family ski trips and Sal had skied in the mountains of upstate New York. She says, "We knew we could get jobs in restaurants so we could work at night and ski during the day. We just wanted to go to Colorado and chill."

But first there was the matter of their future together. Sal never really proposed. They were living together, and they did talk about getting married. They went as far as having their photos taken as a sort of engagement milestone. They talked about an outdoor wedding in Florida. That wasn't going to work for their traditional Catholic parents. Or for their parents' even more traditional priests. There would be a church wedding.

Sal and Cindy moved to Vail for the winter, to return to Louisville for their wedding in May of 1981. Cindy's dad had just sold off his share in his fast-food chain. He was now running for mayor, he would say, to "give back" to the community. Sal and Cindy had loads of restaurant experience, with degrees from a culinary academy. They were about to take their rightful places at the upper level of Louisville's restaurant scene.

At least that was the plan.

CHAPTER 4

The Dreamers Meet Reality

The first thing you do is you make eye contact and then you have a sincere smile and a greeting within the first sixty seconds of them coming in the door. You give them the security that you're going to take care of them. You're wooing this customer to make them feel like, "I matter here."

—Cindy Rubino

I f you had ambitions in the restaurant industry and lived in Louisville, you wanted to work for a Grisanti.

By 1981 the Grisanti family had become a Louisville fine-dining dynasty, complete with corporate feuds and grand expansion plans.

In 1959, Albert Grisanti and his wife, Lilly, better known as "Mamma," decided there was no future in the family business brought over from Italy, making and selling plaster religious figurines (and pink flamingo lawn ornaments). Plastic had started crowding out plaster in the marketplace, and interstate highways were diverting traffic from rural roadside stands. So they turned to another part of their northern Italian heritage—cooking. Brother Ferdinand and cousin Dorina Mattei joined them in combining their skills with food and their sense of ambition that led them to convert the plaster factory into the Casa Grisanti restaurant.

It was a hit, and the family wanted more. Al helped found the Kentucky Restaurant Association, and *Hospitality Magazine* named him to its

Restaurant Hall of Fame. Son Don came home from restaurant school with the idea of adding cannelloni to the menu. Casa Grisanti went upscale in a community hungry for elegance, serving northern Italian dishes and earning national attention. They upgraded the décor, hired a professional chef, and cooked and flambéed tableside. The Mobil Travel Guide gave it Louisville's only four-star rating. *Esquire* magazine listed it among the top 25 restaurants in the nation.

In 1971 Ferdinand left the family corporation and in 1973 opened his own upscale northern Italian restaurant, Ferd Grisanti. By 1977, Casa Grisanti, Inc., opened a second and more casual restaurant, Mamma Grisanti, serving southern Italian fare. Don left the company as his brother Mike took over during a decade of family tension. Disagreements would spill into the media over who deserved credit for the success, how family members treated each other, and the beginnings of an ambitious plan to expand beyond Kentucky.

In January of 1981, Grisanti, Inc., opened a flashy new concept in downtown Louisville, entering the cutting edge of the day's cuisine fashion that brought high-end elegance to traditional American food. The name, Sixth Avenue, Restaurant of the Americas, combined the location of its local intersection with the allusion to New York's Avenue of The Americas. It sat across the street from a brand-new arts center. It offered valet parking. Mesquite charcoal heated the grill, and the menu featured local products as well as influences from around the continent: Native American, Cajun, Maine mussels, Caribbean conch, country-fried ham, cornbread, an oyster bar.

If you had ambitions in the restaurant industry and lived in Louisville, you wanted to work for a Grisanti. And Sal and Cindy Rubino had ambitions.

എ

George Clark had lost his campaign to be Louisville's mayor and had sold his share of Burger Queen, but he kept up his restaurant contacts, and he knew Mike Grisanti well. He vouched for his daughter and new son-in-law. Cindy says, "We had experience. We had four-year degrees from an institution specifically geared toward food and restaurants. They weren't impressed. No, they weren't. They were going to see what we were made of."

Sal talked with George about the Louisville restaurant scene, and decided Casa Grisanti was where he should work.

"I'm like this worldly guy from New York, having lived in Miami, worked in Massachusetts and Colorado, coming to this one-horse, po-dunk town, I'm Italian, this is a slam dunk."

But Casa Grisanti humbled him as soon as he walked in the door.

When he showed up for his initial interview, they kept him waiting for more than an hour. Sal came in to apply for a management position. "They said, 'We don't hire people off the street as managers.'" He got a job as a server.

Cindy landed at the hot new Sixth Avenue restaurant—"as a prep cook in the basement, butchering chickens and gutting fish. They put me in the dungeon and I didn't see the light of day. I'd go in when it was dark and bone chicken upon chicken, whole chickens, and break them down."

℃℈

Louisville sits on the Ohio River. You can walk ten minutes across a pedestrian bridge and be in Indiana. That location shapes its character and its economy—water transportation founded the city. Merchants passing through had to stop there to get around a twenty-six-foot drop over a distance of two miles, a project that got a lot easier after 1830, when locks were built to bypass the rapids. Today you can't look at the river without seeing barges crawling along, and the developed waterfront hosts outdoor concerts and festivals of all sorts. Once a year the downtown bridges close for Thunder Over Louisville, a mid-April fireworks extravaganza launched from river platforms. It's part of the ramp-up to what most people know about Louisville, the first Saturday in May, when the horse-racing world stops for the Kentucky Derby.

When I moved to Louisville twenty-five years ago, I was told two geography-related truisms about the city that seem to get truer ever year.

One came from a native who moved to California and back. Her West Coast friends wondered why she would leave Los Angeles to live in the middle of nowhere. She would reply, "Louisville's not the middle of nowhere; it's the middle of everywhere."

A five-hour drive to Chicago, four to St. Louis, three to Nashville. Ninety minutes to Cincinnati. For a time the *New Yorker* magazine was printed in Danville, Kentucky, two hours down the road. UPS opened a hub in Louisville in 1980 after figuring out that two-thirds of America's cities were within a twenty-four-hour truck drive, and three-fourths of U.S. cities were less than two hours away by plane. Louisville really is the middle of everywhere.

The second bit of wisdom holds that while Kentucky is the South, Louisville is the Midwest. Louisville claims a Southern heritage when it's convenient, like the hiring of women to wear colorful hoop skirts to greet visitors at the airport during Derby week, but from music to theater to dining to politics, the vibe is more middle America than Southern culture. For decades the *Louisville Courier-Journal* ranked in the top ten newspapers in the country. The city has enough hipster pride that you can spot "Keep Louisville Weird" stickers around town, celebrating cultural edginess with the phrase originated in Austin, Texas, and also used in Portland, Oregon.

When Sal and Cindy located from Colorado to Louisville in 1981, it was the United States' 49th largest city, just larger than Birmingham,

Alabama, and just smaller than Omaha, Nebraska. But that doesn't tell the whole story. A lot of people lived outside Louisville but inside the relatively compact Jefferson County—until 2003, when city and county merged to become one new government entity named Louisville Metro. With that single act, by 2010 Louisville Metro jumped to the 17th largest city, behind Fort Worth, Texas, and ahead of Charlotte, North Carolina.

ఴ

So Sal learned he hadn't moved to a one-horse town after all, but the newlyweds did bring abilities that moved them up fast in the Grisanti organization.

The Casa Grisanti style was to wheel the food to the tables on a service cart, where a captain would finish the preparation, put it on a china plate, then hand it to a service assistant who would lay it on the table. Within six months Sal had moved from service assistant to captain. A year after that he moved to Sixth Avenue as dining room manager. In January of 1983 he became manager of Mamma Grisanti's. By 1985 Sal was general manager at Casa Grisanti.

After about six months in the basement, Cindy moved up to preparing cold foods—salads, appetizers, and desserts. When Grisanti added catering, Cindy helped start it, a role with a more flexible schedule that suited her new role as a mom—Salvatore Clark Rubino was born in January of 1983. On the catering team, Cindy worked with a different menu every day, managing a team that decorated the tables, ran the buffet, and arranged the chairs for corporate CEO lunches. "It was exciting," she says.

The years with the Grisantis infused Sal and Cindy with deep and lifelong values of quality and hospitality. The fresh turkey served at The Café today can be traced to Cindy's term in the dungeon.

"Not buying boneless chicken but buying chicken and making it boneless. I don't know that any restaurant does that anymore," says Cindy. Her time in the dungeon added to her food expertise: "I would touch almost every piece of meat that came into our kitchen. If you work that closely with the whole fish, having to break down fish into fillets or peel and devein shrimp, you know instinctively whether it's fresh. You know from the texture or the smell that you need to tell your purveyors that they need to bring you a new chicken. And once they know you'll call them out, they don't send you bad stuff anymore."

Quality was everywhere. "There was no substandard thing. They only bought the top-notch food. Everything had to be a 10. If you overcooked something, you just didn't serve it. There were kitchen inspections to make sure everything on your station was fresh. It was a very disciplined way of operating."

Attention to detail in the kitchen matched the rest of the Grisanti operations. Cindy says, "They laid out the red carpet for the customers. You took care of whatever their desires were."

❧

Sal and Cindy may have absorbed the Grisanti customs, but they literally wrote the book on Grisanti hospitality. Specifically, Sal created a 116-page, loose-leaf three-ring binder of mixed-drink recipes, job descriptions, and policies, complete with illustrations, and instructions like this: "As the service person clears the table, it will be helpful to hold more than one plate at a time…The second plate is placed on top of the knuckle of the thumb and rests on the wrist. It may contact the first plate for stability." Or this: "Clear dishes from the right of the guest with the right hand. Move from guest to guest in a counterclockwise direction…"

Sal says, "They had somewhat of a training manual I decided to update and improve. When the company decided to expand nationwide, they asked me to develop a training manual for customer service employees, dining room employees. I wanted to get ahead, so I welcomed the assignment. I created this handbook that includes the hospitality standards, and I've carried that with me through my career. It's all designed to make sure the guest has a wonderful experience and they want to come back and even recommend it."

The Grisanti restaurants were loaded with talent, from the maître d' to the kitchen, and the organization started to chafe as it tried to spread the southern Italian Mamma Grisanti concept. The restaurants got hurt by downturns in the economy, and by trends toward more casual dining. Staff, including Sal, left to start noted restaurants of their own, accelerating a downward spiral. Sixth Avenue closed in 1989. Casa Grisanti closed in 1991. Mamma Grisanti closed in 1999. Ferd Grisanti closed in 2008.

చ్

In 1987, while Grisanti, Inc., was starting to step out too boldly onto the national scene, work and life were changing for Sal and Cindy as well. In November they had their second child, daughter Lydia. And Sal was growing restless and unhappy in his job. As the Grisanti business worked on developing franchises around the country, he had been looking forward to being a part of the expansion, rising in the corporate ranks to be a district manager. Instead, as manager of Casa Grisanti, he felt he'd been passed over for promotion.

So in thinking about their next career moves, Sal and Cindy dusted off their dreams of owning a mom-and-pop place called Scarborough Fair, and they spread the word that they were open to a new venture. Their networking paid off when a contact, John Locke, called about an available building. Locke would be the landlord and first investor. The next step was to get some business advice from a restaurant expert they knew well— Cindy's dad. And he had an idea.

George knew of a Florida restaurant named Shells that was bringing in crowds by serving large portions of seafood and pasta at low prices in a casual atmosphere. It was pretty much the opposite of a cute lunch café called Scarborough Fair, but George saw growth potential, and he had a proven ability to create an empire. Sal and Cindy would finally own their restaurant, and in a way that would set them up to be financially comfortable, maybe even wealthy. George became a co-investor.

They got to work renovating the building even while Sal still managed Casa Grisanti. They charged hard. They recruited a chef from the Grisantis and sent him to Florida to get a job at Shells, where he learned the recipes and kitchen procedures. Yes they really did that. They named their restaurant Rubino's Sea Shells, at least for a few months, until a cease and desist letter from the Florida restaurant of nearly the same name forced them to shorten the name to Rubino's. "We basically knocked off that restaurant completely," says Sal.

The formula worked.

"It was exciting to be finally on our own," says Cindy. "We'd been in the high end of Italian food, so it was refreshing to have peanuts on the floor and paper baskets for food instead of china and silver."

Cindy took care of the kids at home, coming to the restaurant for quality checks on the food and kitchen operations. Sal ran the restaurant and did the marketing, which was minimal.

"You couldn't afford to spend a lot of money on advertising because you were putting the advertising dollars on the plate by giving large portions," says Sal, a philosophy they've carried through to today. "You would give a lot of food for a low price."

That business model meant high food costs for Rubino's. Sal says that while industry standards for success called for spending less than 35 percent of the budget on food, Rubino's ran at 40 percent.

And that meant customers needed to keep coming even after the opening honeymoon period. One of the ways they put advertising dollars on the plate was with weekly promotions: Sunday was 19-cent oysters, Monday 10-cent peel-and-eat shrimp. Tuesday lobster mania night touted $9.95 lobster, Wednesday $10 king crab. Sal started a weekly morning chat on the air with a radio DJ and got his photo in the local media. It was the beginning of the celebrity chef era. Wolfgang Puck and Emeril Lagasse were getting to be national household names and Sal was getting to be a familiar face around Louisville.

But selling high-volume seafood is different from serving high-end Italian. For one thing, Louisville is more than 600 miles from the nearest ocean. Cindy knew that meant she'd have to be a tough quality cop.

"I would come in and taste these things. Fish, shrimp, oysters, it's so volatile, it has a very short shelf life. You have to have a very fresh product and be right on top of that inventory. You have to fly this in, and if you have a slow day or a holiday or bad weather and it's been sitting there, you have to throw it out and the costs go through the roof. It was pretty demanding."

George found the perfect spot for a second Rubino's. The first restaurant sat about eight miles east of downtown, in a busy area of hospitals and other medical businesses, and a variety of other restaurants—Mamma Grisanti's was just half a block away. This second location was seven miles further east, in a developing area called Middletown. Middletown was made up of a lot of wide-open spaces, but a second beltway around the city had just opened up, and business and housing were about to boom. There was one other cool feature of the second Rubino's location: it was right across the street from the original Burger Queen.

The building was twice the size of the original, closer-in Rubino's. It would have space for executive offices. Two locations would be more efficient—one corporate structure could now earn income from two restaurants. Keeping ambitious restaurant staff called for building a larger organization that would give them a more promising career path.

"I think we saw huge dollar signs," says Cindy. "We were going to be jet-setting around, we were going to be a chain of huge seafood restaurants."

John Locke didn't like the idea. He thought a business should show a profit before expanding, and that hadn't happened. Sal felt torn between his successful father-in-law and the respect he had for the man who gave him his first big break.

The Middletown Rubino's opened in 1991. Business was not as good as at the original store. You couldn't even see it from the street—it hid behind another store. It was near an already-established seafood restaurant. Then Middletown got an Outback Steakhouse, the hot new franchise concept of the day, where customers would wait in line for an hour to get in. In an effort to compete with Outback's popularity, the Middletown Rubino's bought a broiler to add steak to the menu.

The new broiler didn't solve the problem. Customers weren't coming. Cindy saw other signs of unraveling.

"The food was not what it needed to be. I'd check the stations and make them throw things out. Every time I'd go to work I'd just see more problems. The management team was weak. The kitchen team was weak."

Something had to be done. One of the restaurants had to close. Business was better at the original location, but that's the one they shut down.

The rent was cheaper at Middletown, but more important, it held a long-term lease. The original Rubino's didn't.

"We just walked away," Says Sal. "We closed on a Saturday night. Monday morning the doors were locked and the landlord calls us and says, 'What the hell happened here?'"

The wound never healed.

"It was my least proud, lowest moment. It completely destroyed my relationship with John Locke. He disowned me, accused me of not being a man of integrity. It was like a dagger to my heart. It completely destroyed my professional integrity with this man I had earned the respect of, and who gave me my first chance."

It got worse.

Restaurants entertain us by putting on a show when we're off work. That means that for the people who feed us, happy hour starts at ten. Or eleven. Or later.

"You might work a twelve- or eighteen-hour day," says Cindy. "It's very physical, under the stress of the moment, to get the food out to customers; people have been screaming and yelling all night. You've got to go somewhere to unwind, and it's pretty available. There's a bar right there. After the doors are locked, the employees gather around, counting up their tips for the night. The kitchen's breaking down and people start filling up their cups, or they go somewhere else and hang out until four a.m."

Cindy wasn't much a part of that world when the original Rubino's closed in 1992. She was raising a five-year-old and a nine-year-old.

"Being the wife of a restaurant owner is a lonely life," she says. "You've got your restaurant family and you've got your real family. They did a lot of things together there that I was never part of. They'd go out and decompress all their getting through another night of crazy restaurant business. When Sal would finally come home after sixty to eighty hours a week at work, I'd ask things of him as a husband and a father to be part of, and a lot of times it never worked out."

Nothing was working for Sal.

"Everything that was wrong at the restaurant was being blamed on me and my lack of ability or performance." The distance between Scarborough Fair and what was now called Rubino's Steak and Seafood seemed farther than ever. "I wasn't passionate about the concept. I was unhappy with my business. I was unhappy with my marriage. It was life unraveling."

Sal needed to take back control of his life. So, in a move that created family rifts that never fully healed, he quit.

Details had to be managed, of course. Sal formally divested himself of the business—his share was minimal, since John Locke had put up the money. Sal got a job managing a Dairy Queen.

Rubino's still had to be run. Cindy came in to help, along with her brother Dave.

"It was an ugly situation; I'm the daughter and the wife," says Cindy. "It imploded, and Sal left, and my dad had the ball in his court, and I wasn't going to abandon my dad."

Sal moved forward with his plan. He rented himself an apartment a few miles from home, furnished it, and prepared to move in. There was one more step: In August of 1993, Sal asked Cindy for a divorce.

CHAPTER 5

Saving A Marriage

Benedictine Spread
Makes about 20 servings

3 (8-oz) packages cream cheese

3/4 cup cucumber, peeled, seeded, and chopped

1/4 cup yellow onion, diced

1/4 tsp onion powder

1/4 tsp Tabasco sauce (or hot sauce)

1/2 tsp salt

1 drop green food coloring (optional)

Cut cream cheese into chunks and set aside to soften.

Place chopped cucumber and diced onions in food processor. Pulse until smooth consistency.

Add onion powder, hot sauce, and salt to cucumber mixture and pulse until well blended.

Add softened cream cheese chunks to mixture and pulse until smooth. Scrape sides and bottom of bowl, pulse again until smooth.

If desired, add food coloring to food processor. Blend until fine and food color is distributed thoroughly in the mixture, scraping sides if necessary, and pulsing until creamy and smooth. Be careful not to overmix in food processor, or mixture could become too runny.

Chill in refrigerator.

Cindy said no.

In the middle of the chaos of keeping a restaurant running, Sal fracturing the family business, and now getting ready for another food-service job that promised the same long hours, Cindy thought his request for a divorce was mind-boggling. And completely out of the blue.

"We're just trying to survive and now you want a divorce? You're going to work, coming back from work, crashing, going back to work, I had no idea. How did we get here? Bring me back into the loop here. What's going on?"

There was another reason Cindy rejected divorce.

"Part of me didn't want to allow him to have our children without me. I knew the people he was hanging out with and they were not good people. They were living on the edge and I did not want my kids in that environment without me protecting them. 'Are you going to bring these kids into this lifestyle? You're at work all the time.' How would that ever work?"

And there was one more reason. They still loved each other.

After Cindy rejected Sal's divorce request, they agreed to try to save their marriage. They agreed that meant they would have to work at it. What they didn't know was how hard that work would be.

"You think you're going to have this romantic thing, falling in love, and it's just going to continue and it's going to be beautiful, " says Cindy, her words turning hard and adamant. "That fairy tale is a lie as far as I'm concerned. If you don't seek something to grow together, you will just grow apart."

One of the first decisions they made to try to save the marriage was to kill their dream of owning a restaurant.

"When Cindy and I decided to work on our marriage," says Sal, "we agreed we would not be in the restaurant business because we attributed that to our downfall. You have to work crazy hours and you live in this culture of debauchery."

Cindy says, "There's a lot of spousal breakups in the restaurant business because you just can't take the stress of doing it together. It's broken up a lot of marriages that we know."

Sal says, "We knew we needed to reinvent ourselves and not be in that business."

But even that first step of getting their marriage out of restaurants couldn't happen right away. Cindy was still helping her dad at Rubino's. Sal was learning that managing a Dairy Queen offered the same frustrations as any restaurant job, including long hours and demanding bosses.

Sal's Dairy Queen manager job came with a large helping of irony. In a series of complicated corporate deals after Cindy's dad sold his share of Burger Queen, Dairy Queen bought parts of the Burger Queen organization, which by then had changed its name to Druther's restaurants.

The Dairy Queen Sal was managing was located on Dixie Highway, a busy four-lane strip development on the southwest edge of town. The job didn't last.

"That was a disaster," says Sal. "In January we had two and a half feet of snow and the whole city came to a standstill. I got in my little Honda Civic, got stuck in a snowbank, and couldn't get anywhere, so I found a phone and called a taxi. When I got to the Dairy Queen I hired a snowplow and plowed the street. I got the store opened up on time, and my area supervisor was underwhelmed. There was no Uber then, no Google to look anything up on a cell phone, but I got stuff done like a champ and he was like, you could have done more. I quit that job after about a year and a half."

While Sal struggled at Dairy Queen, Cindy worked at a Rubino's restaurant still under a cloud of Sal leaving the family business.

"I stayed in Rubino's with my dad and tried to get it going so he could sell it," says Cindy. "He was not feeling so great about Sal, and I was in the middle. It was awful."

Rubino's added rotisserie chicken and pizza to draw more customers. Cindy helped set up a counter near the front of the restaurant and they named it Sweet Basil Deli. Cindy developed a menu of what she calls "a very simple sandwich line" that would look familiar to patrons of The Café years later: tomato dill soup, sandwiches of chicken salad, tuna salad, and her own version of benedictine, a traditional Louisville cucumber and cream cheese spread said to have been first created in the early 1900s.

Sal and Cindy's future brightened in January of 1995. After his Dairy Queen fiasco he joined a marketing firm. Finally, a nine-to-five job with health coverage. Sal was home evenings; he'd make pancakes with the kids. They leased two new cars. Cindy was pregnant with their third child.

The future darkened again when Sal came home with the news that after four months of not bringing in any new clients, he had lost his job at the marketing firm.

"I'm pregnant and you lost your job. What the hell are we going to do?" Cindy remembers thinking at the time. "It was the bottom of the bottom."

Sal set out to reinvent himself again. He would sharpen his marketing abilities. He joined the Chamber of Commerce to grow his networking contacts. He joined Toastmasters to polish his presentation skills. He thought he might join the ranks of people running seminars for a popular book at the time, *7 Habits of Highly Effective People*. He got a real estate license.

Sal will tell you that through the last half of 1995 he was "grasping at straws." That he was "shaking every tree to see if a bird would fall out."

He thought he could use his restaurant expertise for training and consulting, so he formed a corporation, Hospitality Marketing. He put together a group, including Rick Pitino, who was at the time the revered coach of the University of Kentucky basketball team, to launch a line of pasta called Pitino Foods.

Another of Hospitality Marketing's ventures was a TV show called *Out to Eat*. The production featured short segments on Louisville restaurants, supported by advertising between the segments. One day Sal called on the Louisville Antique Mall—the manager was a childhood friend of Cindy's. Sal asked the owners to sponsor the show. No, we won't buy an ad, they told him, but we would like to have a restaurant in our building.

Sal saw their wish as another straw to grasp at. Another tree to shake. Maybe Sal and Cindy could get back into the restaurant business after all, although he had a pretty good idea of how Cindy would react.

❧

While both Sal and Cindy grew up going to the Catholic church, for them religion was more about the traditions and obligations of an institution rather than an exploration of their faith and spirituality. They attended Catholic elementary schools; young Sal helped his parents run church bingo night. They married in a Catholic church, pleasing both families, and son Clark attended a Catholic elementary school, which was not going well. Clark was bullied, ridiculed, and shoved around by other students, and excluded from activities.

Cindy says the Catholic church "really wasn't working for us."

So Cindy listened in April of 1996 when a family friend invited her to the Good Friday service at St. Paul United Methodist Church, a prominent stone building with a tall bell tower on a busy commercial corner less than a mile away from their house. Several neighbors attended St. Paul, and Clark had joined the Cub Scout troop that met there.

Cindy was at home that Good Friday with eight-year-old Lydia and three-month-old Alex as it rained and thundered outside. "Bring the baby," her friend had said in inviting Cindy to St. Paul. "It'll be fine, we'll go out to dinner afterward."

At the time, St. Paul church was pastored by Howard Olds, a larger-than-life minister known for his dramatic preaching. Sitting in the balcony, Cindy watched as dancers from the Louisville Ballet recreated Jesus's crucifixion story. "It was powerful. It was emotional. It affected me deeply," says Cindy. "I felt I could come to church here."

Later, when Rev. Olds visited the Rubino home, Cindy says, "It touched something in my heart."

Sal and Cindy especially listened to a regular refrain in the Howard Olds sermons. He would say, "Life is fragile, handle with care."

Cindy says, "That spoke to me, because we were feeling very fragile."

❧

The Louisville Antique Mall contained more than 200,000 square feet of retail space on two floors inside an old fabric manufacturing building that sprawled across eight acres between a couple of blue-collar neighborhoods, Germantown and Schnitzelburg, just south of downtown. It opened in 1983, with booths and displays for vendors selling everything from furniture and lamps to jewelry and ornamental Easter eggs to pretty much any kind of knickknack you can think of.

Sal approached Cindy with the idea of running a restaurant at the Antique Mall carefully, casually. "Hey," he said one evening, "I ran into the owner of the Antique Mall, and you know what they want to do? They want to put a restaurant in there, up on the second floor."

"I haven't been down there yet," said Cindy, "but that's probably a good idea. People probably get hungry when they're looking around, and there's not much in the way of eating in Germantown at this point, just a little tavern." Sal saw an opening and took a chance—he proposed that they could run the restaurant.

"I said, 'You cannot make me do that,'" says Cindy. "I fought it tooth and nail because I did not want a replay of what we just went through. We were not doing well financially, but we were better as a unit. I knew what it was going to take from me to build the business. How would we win people over to come there, up the steps and around the corner?"

Here's what Cindy didn't say right away: "At the same time, a subliminal part of my brain said this is exactly what we always wanted to do in the beginning. This is what we said our restaurant would look like. It would be this home-cooking comfort food, all the things we liked to eat, homemade soups, good breads."

Sal listened to Cindy's objections. He told the Antique Mall no, but said he would work with his partners to prepare a space that any food service could move into, and then he would look for a suitable tenant to run a restaurant there. Meanwhile, Sal helped broker a deal to sell George's share in the remaining Rubino's restaurant, ending Cindy's obligation to Sweet Basil.

Sal talked to Cindy again. He listed the reasons that maybe they could run a restaurant together: It wouldn't be permanent, just until Sal could get a real estate business up and running; or maybe the Pitino foods venture would pay off and they could get right back out of the restaurant business; they wouldn't serve alcohol, so the restaurant wouldn't have such a party atmosphere; the hours would be dictated by those of the Antique Mall, 10:00–6:00, but since they wouldn't have a key to the building to prepare and clean up for the day, the restaurant would operate from 11:00–3:00. There would be no late evenings; they didn't have the $75,000 they needed to start up a restaurant, but the Antique Mall owners would co-sign a loan for them.

"It was a crazy, crazy, crazy, crazy idea," says Cindy. "I knew it, but I think I had no other choice. " They had three children, including a newborn, and no job.

So in the summer of 1996, Sal and Cindy Rubino started planning to open The Scarborough Fair Café at the Louisville Antique Mall.

CHAPTER 6

A Little Help from Their Friends

Quick Mac & Cheese
Makes 6 servings

12 oz pasta—fusilli, cavatappi, or macaroni of choice

2/3 cup whole milk

4 slices Deluxe American cheese (not the kind individually wrapped in plastic)

2 Tbsp whipped cream cheese

1 Tbsp Parmesan cheese, grated

1/2 tsp dry mustard

1 tsp Worcestershire sauce

1 tsp chicken base (Better Than Bouillon)

Cook pasta; do not rinse

Combine all ingredients except pasta.

Microwave 2 minutes on power level 6 (or a setting less than the highest—the milk should not boil because the sauce will separate). Stir to combine.

Microwave 30 seconds on high. Stir.

Pour over pasta. Stir to combine.

Microwave 1 minute on power level 6 (less than high).

The first change Sal and Cindy had to make to their dream restaurant was the clunky name. Even before opening, people hearing about Scarborough Fair Café at the Louisville Antique Mall would go, "Huh?" It opened in September 1996 as the less tongue-twisting "The Café at the Louisville Antique Mall."

If the connection with the Antique Mall scuttled the name of Sal and Cindy's dream restaurant, they were literally surrounded by the part of the dream that involved mismatched vintage furnishings. And the logo on the menu featured a drawing of a carousel horse from the descriptions of Scarborough Fair they had talked about in college. White tablecloths with glass tops added a formal touch, and empty cobalt-blue AriZona iced tea bottles made inexpensive flower vases. The banks of fluorescent lights on the ceiling didn't create the kind of mood you want for a restaurant, and there was no budget for lighting. So Sal asked the Antique Mall if he could use some of the light fixtures from the vendor booths. Sure, they said, as long as you keep the price tags on.

"I went into these random booths pulling out lights and putting them in The Café, hooking them up with extension cords. They were for sale, even though people would have to wait until the end of the day to pick them up because you couldn't unhook them with a customer sitting there."

The Café had plenty of wide-open space on the second floor, but Sal and Cindy knew they had to start small, six tables and twelve chairs. It was just the two of them after all, plus eight-month-old Alex. They set up a portable crib in the kitchen, which was small, with just the bare cooking essentials: a four-burner electric stove and oven no fancier than the one in your own home, a small refrigerator, and a steam-jacketed kettle to make soups and sauces without scorching.

With such a simple kitchen, the recipes Cindy brought over from the dishes she developed at Sweet Basil had to be simple and efficient—"menu utilization" they called it back in culinary school. That meant using the same ingredients for different items. The chicken breast in the chicken sandwich was the same one that got diced and mixed with mayonnaise for chicken salad. Spreads made ahead of time helped produce a sandwich quickly. It also had to be good enough to keep people coming back to the restaurant, and telling their friends about it. Cindy combined her love of what she calls comfort foods with her experience of culinary quality, and her sense of combining flavors, along with a phrase her father would repeat from his reading of restaurant trade magazines: the eye eats first.

"All we had to work with were sandwiches and salads. We weren't going to do sauces and decorating the plate, but you can put them together so you can see the layers and the colors and textures. When you build a sandwich, the eye says, 'mmmm this looks like it's going to taste good.' Then when you bite into it, it does taste good because the bread is fresh, the bacon is crisp, the tomato is red, the lettuce is crisp—it's like a piece of artwork. You put the right colors and textures all together in one bite, and it's a flavor explosion."

They named the sandwiches for the periods of the antiques around them: The Early American (roast beef); The French Provincial (turkey and roast beef); The Renaissance (salami and ham); The Queen Anne (benedictine.)

❧

Although Sal had gotten his Realtor license more than seven months before The Café opened, turning it into a viable real estate business came slowly, and that meant juggling two jobs. The Café was just meant to be a bridge to Sal's real estate career, so he would arrive at the office by 7:00 a.m. By lunchtime he was seating customers at the

Antique Mall. After closing The Café at 3:00 for the day, he headed back to the real estate office to make calls and set up evening appointments. He kept his hand in restaurant consulting, mainly working on the plan for a line of Rick Pitino Italian foods.

None of that was bringing in much money.

"We'd been living large with two incomes, and now the creditors were hounding us," says Cindy. "We'd given up our leased cars, we sold a lot of things. We sold antiques, we sold jewelry, whatever we could, just to keep afloat. Sal was very good at telling people our scenario: We've started this business; can you hang on just a little longer; can we send you a partial payment to keep people from putting a foreclosure on our house?"

It broke Cindy's heart that the fears of the parents affected the kids. Clark and Lydia learned the restaurant basics, helping wash dishes and bus tables. They also got an advanced course in the pressure of owning and running a family business.

"The creditors would call and the kids would be at home and they would hear the conversation," says Cindy. "They'd say, 'Is everything going to be OK?' They would see us under the stress of, 'I don't know if it's going to be OK.'" Clark and Lydia learned to tell callers their parents weren't available to talk.

The Antique Mall operated seven days a week and that meant so did The Café. Still, the Rubino family looked forward to Friday. It was the end of the school week. The old Catholic tradition of meatless Fridays, especially during Lent, had been handed down from Cindy's grandmother, to her mom, to her. So Friday meant some kind of fish dinner. In April 1997, Cindy told 12-year-old Clark and 8-year-old Lydia to watch 15-month-old Alex, and she started making a family weekend favorite—salmon croquettes, macaroni and cheese, and peas.

Most of us would pull out a box, at least for the macaroni and cheese. Kraft is plenty good for a non-chef. But Cindy says, "If I have all the ingredients, I can make it taste a little better." She has a recipe for her own Quick Mac and Cheese, and one for salmon croquettes that calls for frying up a blend of canned salmon, crushed Saltine crackers, Worcestershire sauce, and dry mustard and dill, among other additions. Cindy also admits that her decades of practice throwing different ingredients together makes it easier for her to make a more personalized family dinner.

One course of the dinner did come straight out of a package—frozen peas. Cindy started work in the kitchen, assembling her ingredients after putting the peas in a pan of water on to boil, not noticing the handle stuck out over the edge of the stove.

"Alex grabbed that pot of boiling peas and it flipped over on him and the world came to a screeching halt," Cindy remembers. "I literally watched his skin peel off."

The family bundled him through the pouring rain.

"We thought driving would be faster than calling an ambulance, so we loaded up the car and we were praying, we were all crying, and it was a car full of screaming." They had called ahead to the hospital, where "They strapped him to a board and gave him an IV right away to put him out of his pain because he was screaming a scream you never want to hear. None of us will ever forget that scream."

Alex's burns didn't require skin grafts. After five days he came home, with instructions so the family could change his bandages.

Family members still blame themselves for not paying more attention. At the time, they also saw the clear message that they needed to slow down.

"We became more aware of help from the outside, like getting a babysitter to help with the stress on our older children, not putting them in charge," says Cindy. "We decided we needed to sit down and hear about their day rather than jumping into the next thing. We were just building momentum at the restaurant. The word was just getting out that you could go here and have a good lunch, and then this accident happened. We had to get out of the gerbil cage of coming home and immediately going from one thing to the next. We had to sit down, regroup, collect ourselves, and be thankful."

Taking more time for family would get harder. A babysitter would cost money. So would the new medical bills.

A phone call came in from a member of St. Paul church: "What do you need? What can we do? Would you like us to feed your kids? Could we come over and spend the night with your kids? How long are you going to be in the hospital?"

Cindy says the callers visited her in the hospital and they told her about a family injury of theirs at a remote campsite. "They let us know that we weren't bad parents, because you carry that guilt of 'how could I be so negligent?'"

"When we got home, people showed up with food at our door. What? We're in the restaurant business, we don't need to be fed. It was incredible."

Sal scrambled, still looking for a job steady enough to allow an exit from the restaurant business, even as they launched The Café. The family didn't even have a car—a problem in a city the size of Louisville with limited bus schedules, in a restaurant business where meals needed to be delivered and supplies picked up, and a real estate career at a career stage where Sal was trying to do deals all over town. A member of St. Paul church lent him a car for several months until they could finally scrape together $500 for a 1978 VW microbus. The gasket material in the sunroof was worn out so that when Sal accelerated after a rain, water would gush into the back, right in front of the child seat in the back, delighting Alex every time. In other cases, it was more awkward for Sal. He was trying to get his real estate business going, and he was negotiating with investors to launch Pitino Foods. "I remember going to meetings with them and they'd come in with these $100,000 Mercedes and I'm driving this old beat-up little microbus."

❧

The Rubinos had been going to St. Paul for a year and had joined a Sunday school group. It was not the kind of group they were used to.

Clark had started Boy Scouts at St. Paul and needed a pair of hiking socks for a camping trip. "A brand new pair of those showed up inside our front door one day," says Cindy. "Little things like that would happen all the time. I didn't know people cared for one another like that. It was a new way of living.

"There were these deep personal connections. People were just baring their soul and it was like, wow, it was really a huge awakening for us. We hadn't been there long, I felt like you had to earn your way, but this was happening right away. They didn't know if we were good people or bad people. They didn't question why we were Catholic and now we were going to a Methodist church. They didn't question anything. We'd look out on Sunday mornings at The Café and there would be our whole Sunday school class at a long table in the dining room."

When she tells that story more than twenty years later her voice still rises in amazement and her eyes squint and her brow furrows in puzzlement.

"They'd all decided to spend their Sunday having lunch at our business? What's that about? That's crazy. We'd never before felt supported that way."

Revelations

The truth will make you free.

—John 8:32

Proactive people make *love* a verb. Love is something you do.

—*The 7 Habits of Highly Effective People*, by Stephen R. Covey

While Sal and Cindy struggled to build an income for their family, they were also trying to rebuild their marriage, a project of changing their lives that meant meeting with counselors, family, and church members, and looking for what they needed to change about themselves. That introspection brought revelations and "aha!" moments that would take years to become a part of their daily lives. But some of their most significant future habits started with those profound and life-changing flashes of insight.

One of the first of Cindy's revelations came from her dad, who paraphrased a version of a Bible verse.

"It was a tumultuous time," she says. "My dad was going somewhere, we were driving in the car, I was hysterical, crying. Sal had just left Rubino's, leaving my dad with the business, I'm in the middle, my husband's asking me for a divorce, I've got two kids—how was this ever going to work out? My dad said, 'Seek the truth and you shall be set free.'"

The advice from a father trying to comfort his daughter stuck with Cindy.

"My dad never quoted the Bible. I don't know if he even knew it was from the Bible," she says. "I grabbed onto that because so much of what was going on around me was not true. We were not true as husband and wife. We were not truly working in a business together or building a family. There were all these untruths that were happening in relationships, business partners. Nothing was true, it was all fake, pretense, phony.

"It resonated with me that the only thing you can do is to seek what's true and you will not be burdened. I always applied that from then on, asking is this false, is this fake? I started looking for the truth in a situation."

❧

Sal's epiphany took longer to develop. Beginning in 1993, he had evaluated his crumbling life and decided to finish the demolition, to "reinvent myself to become this divorced guy who was going to be out on the scene again and have a whole new life."

He sought validation. When he started going to a counselor, "I wasn't looking to change me. I wanted somebody to understand what was swirling around in my head so they could say to me, 'Oh man, how did you get yourself in this situation?'"

The counselor didn't give Sal the help he'd been hoping for. "She wasn't about to give me permission to divorce Cindy. She told me it was my decision."

And after Cindy rejected his divorce proposal, the counseling continued, but Sal wasn't really getting the message. It was still business as usual as he spent long hours working at Dairy Queen.

"Mechanically, we were working on our marriage, we were seeing counselors," says Sal. "But I was still doing the same thing. I was away from home working all the time, just in a different restaurant."

Sal's "aha!" moment started with a suggestion from a counselor. She recommended a book that was fast becoming one of the most popular business books ever, Stephen R. Covey's *The 7 Habits of Highly Effective People*. You don't have to talk to Sal very long before he'll tell you he almost never reads books, but after quitting Dairy Queen and losing his marketing job, he remembered that book as a way to start a public speaking career. In the summer of 1995 he started training to run seminars that described the seven habits, like "Begin with the end in mind," and "Seek first to understand, then to be understood."

Sal learned the lessons just enough to be able to teach them, but he wasn't applying them to himself. Other projects came up and his public speaking gave way to his *Out to Eat* restaurant show in 1995, and eventually to opening The Café in September 1996.

More than a year after Sal and Cindy first started attending St. Paul church, it was Sal's turn to present a lesson to his Sunday school class. He came up with the idea of dusting off the *7 Habits* teachings he once planned to use as a seminar presenter, and pairing them with Bible scripture. Suddenly a piece of Stephen Covey's advice crackled with relevance: *Proactive people make* love *a verb. Love is something you do: the sacrifices you make, the giving of self.*

"I realized if I wanted our relationship to improve, I needed to act on it," says Sal. "I would have to do things like be a better husband, be a better father, be present in the relationship. I needed to deal with myself, and only by doing that would I be able to be a success with anybody else. What I learned by preparing the *7 Habits* Sunday school lesson was so outside the box, so counterintuitive for me. I was trying to reinvent myself from the outside by asking for a divorce or changing businesses, but I realized I needed to reinvent myself as a better person."

Even with that new insight, Sal would find his reinvention wouldn't happen overnight. It would take years of practice, and still more "aha!" moments.

CHAPTER 8

Second Chances

The Pimita
This gourmet pizza is made with our homemade Pimento cheese, diced tomatoes, bacon, and red onions, with an oversized pita bread for its crust. Accompanied by a cup of "Old Faithful" West Yellowstone Montana Chili. **—menu, The Café**

After taking in only about $50 on its first day, The Café grew slowly, helped by the diners from Sal and Cindy's church. St. Paul church also hired The Café to cater small meetings, and larger jobs, serving dinner for Wednesday night activities, and dinner at an annual post-Christmas pageant.

It all helped a restaurant you couldn't see from the street, that you had to get to by walking through a maze of antiques, and up the stairs. Sal would get on the building's public address system: "Good afternoon, Antique Mall shoppers. Welcome to Louisville Antique Mall. The Café, located on the second floor, is serving lunch until three p.m. Please find your way to the second floor if you get hungry. Today's soup is tomato dill, and our chili is made fresh in-house."

If attracting lunchers to an unlikely spot in an unlikely neighborhood took extraordinary efforts, finding workers to help with the growing business was even harder. "No one wandered in wanting to be a cook or dishwasher," says Sal.

It was Cindy who spotted a source of workers while co-chairing Lydia's Girl Scout troop at Highland Presbyterian Church Nursery and Weekday School. People dressed in traditional clothes from around the world would come in to take English classes upstairs from the Kentucky Refugee Ministries, which in those days was housed in the church. Cindy asked around and learned that Kentucky Refugee Ministries helped refugees adjust to life in Louisville, including finding them jobs.

Sal and Cindy decided to give it a try. In the fall of 2001, an interpreter and a job developer from Kentucky Refugee Ministries brought The Café one of its first job candidates. Marian Reyes (pronounced MAH-ree-ahn race) came from Cuba. She was twenty-five years old, spoke no English, was painfully shy, and had no restaurant experience. Eighteen years later she was still helping run the kitchen at The Café, alongside two sisters-in-law and her mother.

❧

One place to start telling the story of Marian's journey to The Café would be in Moscow on Christmas Day 1991, when the flag of the Soviet Union flying over the Kremlin was lowered for the last time and replaced with the Russian flag. Gone was decades of global power that split the world in a Cold War dominated by an underlying terror of nuclear weapons pointed at each other. Another of the Soviet Union's weapons was known as Comecon, the Council for Mutual Economic Assistance. If the United States was going to spread its influence by helping rebuild the democratic countries in Europe after World War II, the Soviet Union would counter with the Comecon plan to support its allies around the world.

Cuba's geography, just 100 miles from Florida, made it a valued

Comecon member, so the Soviet breakup that ended aid hit the country hard. Oil imports dropped to just 10 percent of pre-1990 amounts, hammering its transportation, industry, and agriculture. Extended power outages became more common. Malnutrition spread. There was even a name for 1990s Cuba: the Special Period in Time of Peace.

Protests over the crashed economy finally couldn't be ignored, so the Cuban government started letting people leave. Tens of thousands headed north in boats, in all states of seaworthiness. In 1994 the US Coast Guard and Border Patrol intercepted more than 37,000 Cubans.

The United States and Cuba made several agreements to manage the crisis. One was a visa lottery in 1994, 1996, and 1998, allowing a limited number of Cubans to become legal, permanent residents of the United States.

Marian Reyes won the lottery. In 1997 she left for Miami with her son and husband.

Marian liked Cuba and still does. She misses it. On vacations she visits family and friends there. In 1996 she liked working there, but her pay was $12. A month. "I needed a better life for my son, for me, my family," she says.

Marian and family made their way to Louisville through Kentucky Refugee Ministries. Early on the morning of September 17, 2001, Marian took two city buses into the dark of a city she didn't know, where people spoke a language she didn't know. She got off at the railroad tracks near the Antique Mall when Cindy pulled up, rolled down the car window, and asked Marian if she wanted to get in.

"She was thinking, 'Am I going to trust her?'" says Cindy. "And I'm thinking, 'Am I going to trust her?' Who are we? I could tell she was overwhelmed."

And Cindy thought, "Would I go to a foreign country and just be dropped off from a bus in a part of town that didn't look too safe and hope I was meeting a good person who wouldn't take advantage of me? That's so scary."

Cindy drove Marian to The Café. Because of the language barrier, "We couldn't really share much, but she was listening to me and trying to do what I showed her to do and I thought, 'Maybe this is going to work.'"

Cindy took a chance on Marian because "I was so burnt out on the typical restaurant worker who thought of their skill set as more than we wanted to pay for and felt they could go down the street and get another job at blah, blah, blah restaurant. 'You want me to do food AND cleanup?' They would come with baggage, like not showing up or showing up late. Habits of coming in hung over. I needed them to be there and be ready to do whatever was needed that day."

In the job interview Cindy asked, "Are you OK with mopping floors?" Cindy would pump her arms in pantomime. Marian would nod and say, "Yes."

"Are you OK with washing dishes? " Cindy would crook an arm and swirl her other hand around inside the imaginary pot. Marian would nod and say, "Yes."

"There was always that willingness to step up to the plate. We both gravitated to get the job done. Some days I would wash the pots and pans; some days she would wash the pots and pans.

"We started building a rapport." Cindy got to know Marian's husband and young son, Ignacio, who Marian was worried about. Marian brought Ignacio into the restaurant, asking Cindy what to do. He had an abdominal hernia bulging from his belly button. On a piece of paper, Cindy wrote the name *Kosair Charities*, a Louisville-region organization that helped kids afford health care.

"She followed up and her son was taken care of," says Cindy.

"We built on that relationship of not only work during the day, but to see to other facets of life. When you come from Cuba, there's no trust there. You never knew who was a spy. You had to be very careful who you talked to. She could talk to me about anything and knew it was going to be okay."

☙

As business continued to improve, so did the need for still more employees. This time a solution walked into the restaurant and sat down.

Pat McKiernan worked around the corner from the Antique Mall as director of alcohol and drug treatment programs for Volunteers of America, a long-time regional nonprofit organization focused on services like addiction recovery and preventing homelessness. Pat's dad would regularly leave his office across the street from Churchill Downs and drive the three miles to pick up his son for lunch. He especially liked a soup-and-half-sandwich combo The Café offered. There were also business reasons for the two of them to meet. Pat worked closely with his dad, who ran Certified Counseling Services. That occupational description doesn't begin to describe Ron McKiernan.

☙

The first line of Ron McKiernan's 2012 obituary reads, "He died sober, a trusted servant." It describes a man who spent a lot of time getting himself, and others, out of trouble and, appropriately, did it with a bit of out-of-the-box drama. The obituary's opening line was Ron's idea and it's also on his tombstone. "It's how he wanted to be remembered," says Pat.

Ron started drinking in third grade. As an altar boy in the Catholic church, he got into the communion wine, and his alcoholism got worse from there, he said in a 2009 story about him the alumni newsletter of his Louisville high school.

Ron got career help from his dad, who headed the International Distillery, Rectifying & Wine Workers Union. He'd get his son jobs in distilleries, "which was paradise for a person like me," said Ron, with a bit of dark humor. When those jobs didn't work out, his dad started grooming Ron for a high-level union organizing position, a short-lived career that included sit-down dinners with Presidents Truman and Kennedy. Ron kept drinking and eventually his dad had to fire him.

Out on his own, Ron says he moved from alcohol to narcotics, selling drugs and robbing drugstores to support his addiction. He got arrested and went to prison. Well, prisons. He served time in penitentiaries in Mexico and the Bahamas, and on a chain gang in Florida.

Ron did have traits that served him well: charm, determination, and creativity.

"My dad was a charismatic guy," says Pat. "People liked having a connection with him. "

While in a prison just outside Louisville in 1972, Ron organized a program around a book by William Glasser titled *Reality Therapy*, which basically describes a counseling technique that, instead of focusing on mental disorders, concentrates on people taking control of their behavior to improve their lives. Ron corresponded with Glasser, who took time out from a Louisville speaking date to visit the prison.

Ron got out of prison and, he says, literally ended up in the gutter. With the help of a couple friends encouraging him, he joined Alcoholics Anonymous. But old crimes followed him.

In 1981 Ron stood in front of a judge in Woodford County,

halfway between Lexington and Louisville in the heart of Kentucky's well-to-do horse country, asking for probation rather than prison after pleading guilty to his second felony of robbing a drugstore. He said he'd been sober for 18 months. He was 44 years old and wanted to be a good citizen and contribute to the community. He told the judge, "I don't plan on being a criminal anymore."

Pat went to the courtroom that day, supporting his dad in his risky strategy of pleading guilty to the charges and asking for probation. He says the judge recessed to talk with the court officers about Ron's request. One by one they opposed probation for this repeat offender: the arresting officer, no; the head of the probation department, no; his probation officer, no; the prosecutor, no.

"The judge says, 'I'm going to do it anyway,'" says Pat. As the group filed out of the room after signing the papers for Ron's release, Pat says he saw the probation officer shaking her head and saying to Ron, "I still can't believe he went ahead and probated your sentence."

"My dad had a way of being able to genuinely express things," Pat says. "I think the judge picked up on his sincerity."

Ron made good on his pledge to live a different life. He got trained as an alcohol and drug counselor and started working his contacts around town to drum up business. One of those contacts was Louisville Mayor Harvey Sloane, and Ron persuaded him to make Louisville one of the first city governments with an Employee Assistance Program. If a city worker got arrested on a drug or alcohol charge, Ron would argue against jail time—they'll lose their job, he'd tell the court. Instead, he'd put them into a treatment program.

"He had all these people getting better in the city system," says Pat. "My dad had an ability to take a really difficult situation and find a path of success through it. He could communicate with people in a way they could receive it. That was a gift of his."

Pat says Ron would use that gift to tell a courtroom why a client of his would be better off with a job rather than in jail. "He could get on the witness stand and explain in a very thoughtful and relatively scientific way why punishment wasn't going to get them where they really wanted to be. 'Do you want this person to not commit crimes anymore? Do you want them to be a productive member of society?'"

Ron eventually spun off the program into his own firm, Certified Counseling Services, contracting with other businesses locally and around the country. He worked with Churchill Downs to start the Thoroughbred Addiction Counseling of Kentucky program. Ron and Pat would run intervention sessions, where friends and family would confront a substance abuser in order to get them into a treatment program.

"He loved it when a family would say, 'Oh, you don't understand. This family member of ours, it's impossible to get them to listen,'" says Pat. "He'd say, 'Oh, they'll listen to me.'

"My dad was really good at saying, 'You're willing to live with all these consequences?' I'd sit there and watch him go back and forth and back and forth. He wasn't going to take no for an answer, and eventually the person gets this look on their face like, he's just never going to stop, and they say, 'Okay, I'll just do what you want me to do.' We'd take them directly to a recovery program. We'd drop them off in treatment and we'd give each other a high five. He was a natural salesman, but what he really wanted to do was sell recovery to people."

Ron's personality also allowed him to turn his passion for recovery into a business that gave him a job.

"He was an energetic guy, he was persistent, he had a high amount of confidence in what he could do," says Pat. "People liked him and they knew they could count on him. If he said he was going to do something, it got done. He could not only sell an idea, he could deliver it.

"My dad was always looking for opportunities."

So naturally, one day Ron got up after lunch at The Café and pulled Sal aside.

"He described his business of a counseling service and asked if I would consider hiring someone who was in the court system. He said if they could get a job and stay working they could avoid jail time," says Sal. "Ron was a larger-than-life character. He commanded your attention and was a good salesman. He was very persuasive. I said, 'Sure I'll give it a shot.'"

But really, Sal wasn't crazy about hiring one of "those people."

"We were willing to try anything at that point," says Sal. "It was difficult to find customers, let alone employees. We needed people, so we weren't going to be picky."

Besides, Sal figured what they needed was a dishwasher—it wasn't like the person they hired would be interacting with customers.

The first hire sent by Ron worked at The Café for a few months. The second changed everything.

"He was the All-American boy next door," says Sal. "He was educated and bright. It totally changed my perspective. These people aren't necessarily homeless derelicts. They can be from an affluent family. They could be your friend's kid, somebody's brother or son. It wiped away that whole stigma and started to open our eyes to the community of people in recovery."

❧

The boy's name is Casey Wagner, and Pat McKiernan says he's "a very good example of what we need to think of when we put a face on someone struggling with substance use disorders. He's the son of a good father and a good mother. He is a product of a community that loves. He suffered from a condition he had no idea whatsoever that he had until he had it.

"By expecting him to show up as a derelict, Sal expressed a common misconception. We tend to put an ugly, hateful, and fearful face on addiction until we meet someone in early recovery and we realize they're somebody's son or daughter; that they came from a family with a value system; that they possess qualities that you would want to have in your business."

That's common knowledge among drug and alcohol counselors, but not always to the rest of us. One journalist who studied addiction after his son nearly died is David Sheff. He wrote the book about his experience that became the movie *Beautiful Boy*. He wrote another book more broadly about addiction titled *Clean: Overcoming Addiction and Ending America's Greatest Tragedy*. The first paragraph of its preface reads in part: "Using drugs or not isn't about willpower or character. Most problematic drug use is related to stress, trauma, genetic predisposition, mild or serious mental illness, use at an early age, or some combination of those. Even in their relentless destruction and self-destruction, the addicted aren't bad people. They're gravely ill, afflicted with a chronic, progressive, and often terminal disease."

That was Ron McKiernan's world, says Casey Wagner.

"Ron loved alcoholics and convicts," says Casey. "His life's mission was to get people out of jail that he knew were in there because they had an addiction. He knew that because that's who he was. He is a Saul to Paul, for a Biblical reference. I've never met anyone like him. I never will meet anyone like him."

❧

Casey Wagner earned straight A's and ran cross-country at Trinity High School, a prestigious Louisville Catholic school in a trendy part of town. He earned an academic scholarship to the University of Dayton in Ohio. But when his mom and her sister dropped him off at college, "There was a feeling of impending doom," says Casey.

"My dad actually did not want me to go to college. He wanted me to withdraw and go into treatment that summer because I had been caught with cocaine. My dad thought, this isn't just a kid who's drinking a beer or smoking a joint every now and then. He's developed a serious addiction. I felt bad because I knew deep down my dad was right."

ॐ

Casey can't give you a reason that drug and alcohol use took over his life.

"I don't know why," he says. "Alcoholics will share stories that we felt like something was missing in our life. We didn't feel good enough, smart enough, strong enough, cute enough. Alcohol gave us that sense of completion and drugs would further heighten it, that sense of euphoria, that artificial self-esteem. But I think every teenager has self-esteem issues."

Part of the reason could be predisposition. People who study addiction say genes can influence a range of traits, from how long a drug stays active in the bloodstream to tendencies to be influenced by peer pressure. That was not news to Casey's parents. They had both been in recovery from alcoholism for years. They had remained sober ever since Casey was born.

Casey got caught smoking pot when he was thirteen. By fifteen he was habitually drinking by himself. He held different jobs in restaurant kitchens through high school and was a valet parker for a high-end downtown restaurant until "I got fired from that job. Evidently they don't want you to be drunk when you're parking expensive cars."

On that first day at the Dayton campus, Casey says, "We went to buy my textbooks and I had no money. I had completely burned through all my graduation money and my savings," he says. "That's usually indicative of a drug problem. They never have any money in their account. They're always overdrawing to get their next fix."

"I had to ask my aunt to buy my books for me and there was this look of real disappointment. A light bulb went off in my mom's head and I saw it. It was the first step of me feeling the guilt, shame, and remorse. I realized I'd let her down because she'd been advocating for me with my dad."

Casey got a job in the dorm cafeteria and "I got fired the second day because I showed up to work so messed up." He went to the phone book and looked up Alcoholics Anonymous and attended a few meetings. But on St. Patrick's Day he took some hallucinogenic mushrooms. To ward off a bad trip, he got a hold of some illegally bought anti-anxiety medication and took the whole bottle. He got taken out of his dorm room on a stretcher and to the emergency room, where they pumped his stomach and otherwise worked to save his life. Once they figured out he wasn't going to die, Casey says, the police came in and started interrogating him. Within a week he was gone from the school. His mom took him to a treatment center in Louisville.

A few weeks later, he vanished for "one last binge," smoking crack and "running the streets." He got pulled over by the police, who for some reason didn't search his car, where they would have found drugs and alcohol. At one stop he saw two men he knew from an AA meeting and felt he needed to hide his face from them. The close call with the police and the shame of trying to avoid friends from recovery started him realizing how far he had fallen from a sustainable life.

Casey's parents, he says, were "absolutely fearing for my life." They knew they needed to take a more desperate step with their son, so they turned to a family friend who they knew from their own recovery community—Ron McKiernan.

Casey returned to the treatment program ready to confess that he'd gotten high that weekend. But something was different.

"I saw that Ron was in there," along with other family members, says Casey. He wasn't close with Ron, but he knew enough about him to realize, "Oh man, I'm in trouble."

In the intervention, Casey's parents took back the things they were paying for—his cell phone, his car keys, his house keys. They pointed out that meant he was now homeless.

"I broke down and started crying. I said, 'I'm done.'" Without even packing, he walked straight to Ron's car. "I cried all the way down to detox."

The Healing Place is a residential treatment center in downtown Louisville. Near the front is an open room just for detoxing, sparely furnished with beds placed about four feet apart. A bulletin board holds haunting Polaroid photo reminders of faces of people who did not survive recovery. Casey calls his seven days there "horrifying. I don't remember a whole lot about it. Your brain is so jittery and foggy. It was hell."

He does remember standing for a smoke in a fenced-in area and thinking, "How the hell did I get here? About a year before that, I was graduating from Trinity, about four blocks from there, in my white tux, wondering when I zigged when I should have zagged. It took me a long time to realize it was a series of zigs, not just one."

Ron's recovery plan for Casey took him to residential recovery houses, and eventually to a job where others in treatment worked, helping lay carpet for a flooring company. Casey got laid off regularly during the slow winter months, and a high school knee injury made it tough to handle the task of kicking the carpet into place. One day Casey stopped in to The Café for lunch and ran into a friend from an earlier restaurant job who was now working for Sal and Cindy—a friend who would vouch for him if he wanted to work there. Casey wrote up a proposal to apply for a job at The Café and submitted it to a session of his group therapy.

"Ron surprisingly approved it," says Casey. Ron warned him not to try to pull anything over on him.

There was good reason for concern about returning to a restaurant job.

"The restaurant industry is known as a place where a lot of people have drug and alcohol problems because it promotes that lifestyle," says Casey. "If you're only working a night shift, you have a lot of cash in your pocket from tips. You get off work, you drink and drug and you don't have to get up until noon the next day."

Casey figures Ron approved his proposal because The Café only served lunch. And because it was near the Volunteers of America offices and its halfway houses, where Ron could meet his son for lunch.

"I'd see him in there for lunch all the time after I started working there," says Casey. "I think he was spying on me."

Casey agrees his job interview might have helped Sal see addicts differently.

"I'm the same age as his son," says Casey. "I think that resonated with Cindy and Sal."

☙

"I loved working at The Café," says Casey. He fit in quickly, got raises, and learned. He started washing dishes, then helped make sandwiches. He learned some Spanish from the other kitchen workers. Cindy taught him to make cakes. Compared to his life before, he liked the continuity of having a job. After about two years, he ran the kitchen on weekends.

He especially liked the perk of a free lunch when you worked a full shift. He says almost every day he ate the Pimita, a pimento cheese pizza on pita bread. He'd throw on banana peppers and black olives and eat it with a Coke.

Casey was also attending the University of Louisville's J.B. Speed School of Engineering, and his day job was getting in the way of his studies. After an emotional goodbye, he left The Café for work at Volunteers of America, where he could work at night.

His schooling included an internship at a Louisville plant of Alcoa, the aluminum manufacturer. He graduated with a degree in chemical engineering and moved to another Alcoa plant near Knoxville, Tennessee, as an environmental engineer. In 2010 he moved to work in corporate strategy at Alcoa's main office in Pittsburgh, where he earned an MBA from Carnegie Mellon University.

Casey's dad was diagnosed with terminal cancer. Casey was married by then and they both wanted to be closer to home, Casey in Louisville, his wife, Katie, nearer to home in Knoxville. Casey found a job at GE appliances in Louisville, buying raw manufacturing materials.

"I've been sober now for seventeen years," said Casey when I interviewed him in the summer of 2019, rapping the tabletop with his knuckles for a good luck wish. He'd been married for six years, had a year-and-a-half-old daughter, Dolly Faye (after Dolly Parton, he says), and was expecting a second child. When I observed that he sounded like a success story, he teared up.

Casey said he often thinks about a friend he knew years ago from detox, who he's seen in his neighborhood, still losing to addiction.

"He's dying," says Casey. "A lot of times I wonder why it's me that's here. For whatever reason, I've had a lot of people help me along the way. It's a success story that I've played a part in. I know a higher power has played a part in it. I know that many other people have played a part in it, like Cindy and Sal, Ron McKiernan, my parents. And there have been other people who have not been so lucky."

Casey's mom has been sober since two years before he was born. Nanette Mershon recognized early that she had a family history of alcoholism. While visiting a relative in a treatment program, a counselor convinced her to start attending a recovery program. As a result, she says, she avoided the wrenching and life-threatening journey of many addicts. "I never had to hit bottom."

Mershon says their background in recovery allowed her and her husband to help with Casey's treatment. They knew Ron McKiernan from groups they'd been in. "Give me your son," he told them.

"I was so lucky I had been in a program and knew people," she says. "I had this bucket of knowledge and so many people don't have that."

When Ron and Casey left the family intervention to go to the detox center, Mershon knew the program called for a long time in treatment centers and halfway houses with no contact with the family. "I understood that, but I thought I should be an exception. I had to do so much letting go."

She would cheat when she could, mainly by sneaking into The Café.

"I would go eat there just to see him," she says. "I knew I had to really be careful because if Ron knew I was going down there he would have killed me."

She says, "I remember Sal coming to my table a couple of times and he'd say, 'You have a great son.' I still go in there and shake his hand and say, 'I'm Casey's mom.' He gave Casey a job. I owe this guy my arms, my legs, my heart, everything."

CHAPTER 9

Lessons From the Kitchen
and the Mountaintop

I wanted them to see we were who we said we were.

—Cindy Rubino

Cindy decided to take her business dilemma to church.

Income was still precarious. Every day Sal and Cindy worried about losing their house. But things were picking up at The Café. More and more people were lunching there, enough so they had hired experienced kitchen workers. Cindy was able to take some time off for herself and the family, but something was not right. When she would return to work she'd hear stories about fights and bullying. Marian didn't seem to be part of the problem; maybe Cindy could give her more responsibility. But Marian didn't have a restaurant background, and she still could barely speak English.

Through St. Paul church Cindy and Sal heard about something called the Emmaus Walk, named after the Biblical story about an encounter with Jesus. The Emmaus Walk is a weekend retreat that started in the 1960s with the Catholic church and later was adapted for Protestant churches. The format brings a group of church members together with the aim of integrating their faith into their everyday lives. Cindy thought that was just what she needed.

"I came to the Emmaus Walk with that question," says Cindy. "Who should I rely on to help run the restaurant?"

Cindy describes her experience at that Emmaus Walk as being "poured out on all weekend long by people who want to care for you and meet your every need, and hearing stories of other people who've gone through hardships and have found true meaning in their life through finding Christ. It opened our eyes to where we needed to be, and I had this question the whole time that weekend: I'm at a crossroads trying to find people to help me at The Café."

Cindy saw the choice she needed to make as a business decision, but also as a moral decision.

"We're not going to make fun of other people at work," she concluded. "We're not going to harass other people here. This is a community and we're going to care for one another."

"I came back away from that weekend knowing I had the answer," says Cindy. "Marian is going to be my number one person."

Marian, Cindy says, "seemed more on track with my heart."

Cindy returned from the Emmaus Walk to The Café with the resolve that, "I'm going to work side by side with her and we're going to figure this out. It worked great. Marian reacted like, you're investing in me? Whoa, I'm stepping up to the plate because this is my opportunity. She started picking it up and taking it on."

❧

Cindy says the secret to keeping an employee like Marian for more than eighteen years is trust—an especially deep version of trust that sees a person rather than just an employee.

"I always said if I had a place where I could run my kitchen I would run it fair and honest and treat people with dignity," she says. "I wanted them to truly trust me and believe in me that I wasn't going to abandon them in trying to get this restaurant off the ground. I wanted them to know that if there were any issues with children or spouses sick, we always said, it's no problem, you go take care of them, we'll pick up the slack. I wanted them to know that first was your family and then came your job.

"I wasn't treated like that," she says. "In the restaurant business it was about the job and it was cutthroat when we learned the business—okay, if you don't do this you don't have a job, you're outta here, we've got somebody else who will take your place."

Cindy says she would make a point of demonstrating teamwork.

"We couldn't afford to have a whole other crew come in and clean at the end of the day, so I always said I'm going to take the hardest job that nobody wants to do—pot scrubbing, pushing a heavy industrial-size mop. I wanted them to truly trust me and believe in me. I wanted them to see we were who we said we were."

That statement sums up the essence of The Café's management success. It explains the hard-nosed practicality of combining decency, spirituality, and integrity, that last word being defined by *The American Heritage Dictionary* as "being whole or undivided." Cindy needed to keep good workers but couldn't pay top dollar or offer the cushiest working conditions. Showing "we were who we said we were" meant "we didn't have an agenda to put demands on people we weren't willing to put on ourselves."

After an exhausting day of serving food, Cindy says, "I would have to say okay, now we're going to scrub this place down so that tomorrow morning we can come back in here and do it again. And again, and again. A lot of people will say, 'I can work somewhere else for the same amount of money,' so I had to get people to buy into that we're going to provide a place for you every day to come in and earn a living, and we're going to be working right alongside of you. I would be the last person to leave, so they knew I was committed, and we respected each other for that. Sal and I had to create that environment to keep the people we wanted to keep."

∾

Emmaus Walks aren't supposed to end after the three-day weekend. Groups are supposed to stay in touch. For Sal, that meant he would still be meeting with two other men years later, for breakfast every Thursday. For Cindy, it was a way to make her faith a part of her life and work. And it would begin to form The Café's practice of how it treated its employees, including deliberately hiring refugees and people in recovery from alcohol and drug addiction—giving people a second chance at life.

"These Emmaus Walk groups started holding us to another level of accountability daily. What do Christian values look like?" says Cindy. "Christian values are treating others like you would want to be treated, whether they speak the same language, were raised in a different culture, or worship in a totally different way than us. We're all God's people."

The Emmaus Walk, Cindy says, "was a pivotal point in our lives. Sal and I felt like we were given a second chance in life to really understand the bigger picture of how to live your life in connection with God. Offering a second chance to benefit someone else came to be something we would want to develop in our business."

For Sal, hiring refugees and people in substance recovery wasn't a matter of faith or a plan to do the right thing. At least not at first.

"We were just trying to fill positions," says Sal. "It was total business. But when we looked back we realized it was God at work.

"It happened organically. It wasn't something we set out to do and create a business plan for. We found it happening to us and we tried to be open and listen to God's will in our life. We felt we were being led, so when we were introduced to the refugees and were introduced to the people in recovery we felt like, we've gotten a second chance, we got this business going, we've got this income stream. Why not give these people a second chance? People want to give us the credit, and I say, 'We didn't do this. God did this in our life and these people changed our perspective.'"

That perspective helped The Café succeed, says Cindy. Refugees and people in recovery have traits that make them good employees. Sal and Cindy discovered that addicts in a recovery program, unlike other job applicants, "had someone to go talk with to keep them from going off the deep end. They showed up for their job because they didn't want to be homeless again."

"Refugees," says Cindy, "are focused on their second chance. They want to make the most of it for their family. They want to move on to getting their citizenship, they want to move on to buying a home, getting a driver's license. They have these benchmarks they want to grab on to. There's nothing harder than living in a refugee camp. This country, this business, is not hard to them."

Giving people second chances, says Cindy, "is good business. We wouldn't be here if we hadn't hired the people who were willing to do the entry-level jobs and stay."

સ૭

John Koehlinger would say Marian Reyes is not technically a refugee, since she came to the United States not by requesting asylum, but through a specific agreement between the United States and Cuba. But she was fleeing oppressive conditions, and unlike many immigrants who move for a job, to be with family, or to join others who came from her country or community, she knew no one in Louisville.

Koehlinger is executive director of Kentucky Refugee Ministries, a Louisville-based organization that helps refugees come to the United States and become part of American society. It is one of nine resettlement agencies of the Church World Service, a 70-year-old organization that helps resettle migrants and refugees. Since Kentucky Refugee Ministries started in 1990, it's helped resettle more than 16,000 refugees. It's housed in a large, sprawling building full of meeting rooms, classrooms teaching English and other skills for life in the United States. A staff of more than 80 caseworkers, teachers, and immigration attorneys oversee refugee resettlement work, including coordinating more than 600 volunteers, and making sure refugees coming to the United States are properly credentialed. Kentucky Refugee Ministries will typically partner with a Louisville community group, often a church, to find housing and a job for people arriving from other countries, and welcome them in other ways, including organizing groups of people to meet arriving refugee families at the airport. The agency works with some 200 Kentucky businesses interested in hiring refugees, including The Café.

Koehlinger credits The Café with giving Marian, and all the refugees it hired after her, more than a job. He says that when refugees first arrive in a new country they can look and feel like outsiders.

"People see them in an apartment complex or riding the bus, they're speaking a different language, they're wearing different clothes, their kids get bullied in school," says Koehlinger. "Sal and Cindy were some of the first friends, mentors, people who trusted them. Refugees spend so much time working that the rapport they may or may not have with their employer is important in their quality of life, their feeling accepted and valued. Sal and Cindy cared about those women on a personal level. Cindy was like their caseworker, their mentor, their mother."

Koehlinger believes Sal understands the business value of those close-knit relationships.

"He's always quick to give the employees credit for the phenomenal success of that restaurant. Even though people don't see the refugees back working in the kitchen, he always mentions that The Café wouldn't be as successful without them, that they helped build the restaurant. It's a family kind of atmosphere."

Koehlinger regrets today's conditions that reduce the number of refugees coming into the United States, even as an expanding economy in 2019 made employers more willing and able to offer jobs to refugees. Official limits lowering the numbers allowed in, as well as slowdowns in processing applications, have cut the numbers being resettled by Kentucky Refugee Ministries from about 750 in 2016, to as few as 250. Accepting refugees doesn't just save them from danger and oppression, he says, it also benefits the United States.

"Refugees are very grateful for the freedoms and legal rights and protections they have here and extraordinarily proud to be American," says Koehlinger. "Some people who are born here take for granted what that means, but refugees who have been deprived of those basic rights and freedoms appreciate them keenly. They don't take anything for granted."

One member of the Kentucky Refugee Ministries board who's watched The Café's hiring practices pay off is Jason Crosby, pastor of

Crescent Hill Baptist Church, which has a history of members who are refugees. Crosby agrees that Sal and Cindy's management style, and the kind of work a restaurant requires, has helped refugees adjust to life in the United States.

"The Café is kind of a magical place in that it's not a factory. It gives you the opportunity to engage and interact with other people. To work on your English," says Crosby. And he sees a business edge.

"A lot of other employers hired these folks because they're cheap, relatively unskilled labor. Sal and Cindy understood these folks were not unskilled. They saw the refugees' gifts and talents that other people did not see."

☙

One of the business ventures Sal was trying to get started, Pitino Foods, ended after September 11, 2001. Rick Pitino's brother-in-law, who the basketball coach considered his best friend, was working on the 105th floor of the second of the twin towers to collapse in New York City that morning. A startup business venture was one thing too many for Pitino, who was by then coaching the University of Louisville basketball team. "He was like, I'm done, I can't do this," says Sal.

The loss of Pitino Foods wasn't the setback it might have been for Sal's business plans. It was just one of the straws he was grasping at toward the goal of building enough income to exit the restaurant business. The Café was starting to catch on and Sal was building a reputation as a Realtor.

Repairing their marriage was a different story. Trauma lingered after the Rubino's restaurant breakup, the near-divorce, family and financial stress. Sal had his *7 Habits* insights about working to change himself, but his day-to-day behavior was still a work in progress. Then Sal found a new revelation when he went to the mountaintop, figuratively and literally.

❧

Cedar Rock is a 4,000-foot-high mountain with spectacular views of the surrounding Appalachian Mountains in western North Carolina around Asheville. You don't have to start at the bottom in order to climb the whole height to get to the top. A drive through the mountains will take you to a trailhead that's already partway up to the summit. But hiking the rest of the way is no stroll. The trip goes up a lot of sometimes-steep bare rock—at one point the trail rises 270 feet over just a quarter mile.

In the fall of 2003, Sal and Cindy's oldest son, Clark, was nearing the end of his college years with a semester at Castle Rock Institute, not far from Cedar Rock. Sal grew up spending time in the Catskill Mountains around Newburgh, and Clark had earned Eagle Scout status. The people, the place, and the timing seemed ideally aligned for a father-son outing. Still, other circumstances came together to make way for another "aha!" moment in Sal's life: there was the obvious analogy to a mystical mountaintop experience, and he would be making the journey accompanied by a son with an especially strong Christian faith.

Sal says that, over the years, Clark and Lydia's involvement in St. Paul church had made them spiritual leaders of sorts to their parents. He says Clark was especially consistent in his faith, going on to earn a degree in religious studies.

Cindy noticed Clark's faith early, especially one day during elementary school when he adapted the Bible verse, "Forgive them, for they know not what they do," to his own everyday routine.

"He became a victim of bullying right away because he was a very mild, meek kind of kid," says Cindy. "They bullied him on the bus, they bullied him on the playground, but he told me one day, 'Mom, God will forgive them because they don't know what they're doing.' I couldn't believe it was coming out of his mouth. I was like, you remembered that? He was only five or six years old. I was floored that he took that and applied it to his life. He's always been that kind of deep thinker."

Sal set out for Cedar Rock, headed south for the five-hour drive to bond with Clark that October day in 2003, along with the family dog, a Jack Russell Terrier puppy named Ty. Father, son, and dog would camp at the base of the mountain, then head up to take in one of the world's better views of the sunset.

Sal got worried right away. His nearly 50-year-old body felt the altitude, incline, and terrain. Clark had researched their route, even to the point of hiking it himself with a couple of outdoor adventure specialists a few weeks earlier. Ty scampered with them up the rocks, but Sal was feeling it. He didn't tell Clark he was getting scared. He was determined that this would be great quality time with his son.

They reached the summit, sitting to rest and take in the vista. Clark suggested they walk around and explore the clearing at mountaintop, but Sal had another agenda.

"There has to be another way down."

He finally confessed to Clark that he was frightened about heading back down the steep rock.

Clark explained, from the benefit of his research and experience, "No, Dad, everyone I've spoken with has told me that the only way up or down Cedar Rock is the rock face."

Sal found a path heading down. Clark followed. After a few feet the trail turned into impassable thorns and thickets. Sal found another way down, leading to another dead end. By now they'd missed the planned viewing of the sunset. Worse, they hadn't packed flashlights.

"Dad, we need to just go down the rock face," Clark said, and reassured him, "You'll be okay. It's getting dark. We shouldn't waste any more time."

"Let's try one more trail," said Sal. With the third failure, he gave up.

Clark again tried to calm his dad. "You're going to be fine. I'm right here with you. I'll go down first and mark the spots." They returned to the top of the rock face as the last sliver of sun disappeared and the full moon lit up the rocks below. Clark led both of them in a prayer for their descent. The trip up earlier in the day had taken about twenty minutes; going back down took about thirty, carrying Ty part of the way. But they made it off the mountain.

On the drive back to Louisville with Ty in the passenger seat, Sal pulled the car over and started crying.

He suddenly saw the hike as a metaphor for the mistakes in his life. He had been living as though he always knew best, and that there was always an easier way. A shortcut. He didn't have to do the hard work of climbing down sheer rock, or of considering that maybe he was wrong and the other person was right. On a hike, maybe he should listen to his son. In his marriage, maybe he should be listening more to his wife. In his life, maybe he should listen to what God was telling him.

"It was an awakening," says Sal. "I keep running into the wilderness and getting scratched up only to find out I've still got to go and do the hard thing. I realized I needed to surrender and be obedient."

It had been ten years since Sal had asked Cindy for a divorce; it had seemed the easy way out. Instead they had decided to do the harder work of keeping their marriage together. At Cedar Rock Sal faced another sign that the easy way isn't always the right way.

Stopped on the side of the road, he phoned Cindy to describe his awakening. But Cindy hadn't been to that mountaintop.

"I was probably in the midst of something and I said, 'Oh that's great. I'm sorry, but I'm thankful you're okay and it ended up being a good trip,'" she recalls. But if she didn't share the emotion of Sal's epiphany, she had her own way of seeing its significance.

"It was where we were in our lives that we would have these monumental moments of understanding," she says. "Sal was always looking for a way to take the side route. It was a very self-aware moment for him to say 'don't try to find a shortcut.' There's not a quick answer to life. You've just got to get in and dig it out. He realized you don't take off and go rogue with your agenda. You look at the bigger picture because that might affect other people. It was his 'aha!' moment when he realized, 'I'm weak and I'm flawed.'" Sal would turn Cedar Rock into a PowerPoint presentation, reporting the lessons to his Emmaus Walk group. Cindy saw another angle to that side-of-the-road call from Sal, one that showed hope for their marriage.

"For me, it was that he shared his realization with me," she says. "He could have just said, 'Oh, man, I almost screwed that whole thing up.' But rather than keeping it to himself, he called to tell me."

They would need hopeful signs, because another test loomed for their marriage, family, and business. The Café's lease with the Antique Mall was just about up, and Sal couldn't get a clear answer from the owners about whether they would renew.

CHAPTER 10

Never Again On Sunday

Cindy's Amazing Bread Pudding
Makes 10-12 servings
[Note: before baking, bread mixture must soak overnight]

1 cup granulated sugar

1 cup brown sugar

1 tsp cinnamon

1/2 tsp nutmeg

4 eggs, blended together using
  wire whisk

2 cups milk, whole

2 cups heavy whipping cream

2 tsp vanilla

1 Tbsp butter to grease baking dish

8 cups day-old French bread, cut into 2-inch pieces, pressed and compacted
  into measuring cup

1/2 cup raisins (optional)

Orange-Butter Sauce (recipe follows)

whipped cream, optional (garnish)

1. Put both sugars and spices into large bowl. Add eggs, milk, cream, and
    vanilla; blend ingredients using wire whisk until sugars are dissolved.

2. Place bread in generously buttered 13x9x2 baking dish.

3. Pour mixture over bread, dispersing evenly, pressing it gently with a perforated spatula until all bread is well soaked. If desired, spread raisins over top and incorporate into mixture.

4. Cover with parchment paper and aluminum foil, crimping edges well to make good seal. Refrigerate overnight.

5. Next day: Preheat conventional oven to 375° (or 350° for a convection oven).

6. Remove baking dish from refrigerator and let sit on counter for 15 minutes.

7. Bake, covered, on middle oven rack for 80 minutes (60 minutes for a convection oven).

8. Remove from oven. Remove covering and bake, uncovered, an additional 10 minutes until golden brown.

Orange-Butter Sauce

1/2 cup butter

1/3 cup granulated sugar

2 Tbsp frozen orange juice concentrate

1 tsp pure vanilla extract

1/2 cup sour cream

In a medium saucepan, melt butter over a low heat.

Add sugar, orange juice concentrate, and vanilla; stir over low heat until well dissolved.

Turn burner off; stir in sour cream with wire whisk until it's a smooth, velvety consistency.

Spoon as desired over top of warm bread pudding when serving. Garnish with whipped cream as desired.

Cakes became a signature of The Café. Towering, foot-tall, ornately frosted creations. The Tuxedo Cake topped with that shining ganache that looks like liquid chocolate and crowned with a wreath of cream cheese icing; the strawberry cake dressed with half slices of its namesake fruit; the glaze of gooey coconut frizz on the German chocolate. Those were the three basic cakes, plus a cake of the day. And there they were, sitting on a table at the front door, three of the structures, with slices out of them so you could see the layers inside, in your face before you could even tell the greeter how many were in your party. And when you did order, the server laid in front of you a slice so generous no one could eat it by themselves.

The cakes as a feature of the restaurant started while Cindy still worked at Sweet Basil, when Rubino's was frantically trying to remake its seafood formula with a new grill, rotisserie chicken, pizza oven, and a refrigerated display case of cakes up front, following Cindy's dad's rule of "the eye eats first."

Rubino's cakes came from a high-end bakery too expensive for The Café's more modest resources. Dessert at the Antique Mall was a cookie or lemon bar. Until Cindy came up with her own version of bread pudding.

"I never had bread pudding growing up. My parents talked about it, and I always thought it sounded awful. Why would bread taste good as a pudding?" Cindy's dad would tell her that when he was growing up, bread pudding was a substitute for cake, which they couldn't afford. His mom would make it out of leftover biscuits. As The Café was getting started, so was the Food Network on cable TV, and with it, attention to different cuisines, including southern food, like bread pudding, for example. Cindy rethought her attitudes toward bread pudding—if it was a cheaper cake substitute for her dad's family, maybe it could work that way at The Café. Cindy took the same blend of practicality and creativity that made the family's traditional bread pudding and updated it for the new interest in retro and regional cooking.

"I started thinking about comfort desserts, and I thought, bread pudding is very Southern. I started looking up recipes and I thought, we have French bread left over every day," she says. "I wondered what kind of custard could you make that soaks overnight? Everybody had bourbon sauce. I felt bourbon didn't reflect who we were at the time. We didn't have alcohol on the menu. I liked citrus, so we did an orange sauce."

Still, even with the addition of bread pudding to the menu, she kept thinking about cakes. "We wanted to make a statement with dessert."

They heard about a friend of a friend who made special occasion cakes in her home. That more affordable solution worked for a while—they were smaller than what the cakes at The Café would later become, but they were good enough to develop a reputation, and even at first they advertised themselves by sitting on covered, raised stands near the door. When the baker couldn't keep up with both family and business anymore, Cindy again had to learn more about cakes. Marian was managing the kitchen by then, so Cindy could spend time "building my repertoire."

For one cake she reached back to the kitchen of her mother's mother.

"Our strawberry cake was my grandmother's recipe. She always made it for me growing up because I have a July birthday, when strawberries were in season. She'd go pick the berries and make a cake with them. It would have strawberry icing. It was like a bite of summer," says Cindy. "She hadn't given me the recipe, so I said, 'I'm going to figure out how to make my grandmother's strawberry cake.' It took me a while to get it just the way she made it, and then I did it. That's exactly what it tasted like."

And it's not just the appearance of the cakes at the entrance that makes them so memorable. It's also how they're served.

"People always say, 'you serve the biggest slices of cake,'" says Cindy. "It's our advertising. Everybody sees somebody get a piece of cake at the table, another table sees it, it sells itself. It's developing that excitement, that anticipation of getting something that's more than you deserve at that price."

Servers slice the cake when it's ordered," Cindy says. "They just look better, they're fresher. You're getting a piece of cake sliced right in the moment, which means it ends up being a bigger slice. We lose at least two pieces out of every cake that way, but the marketing you create is priceless. You create this whole chatter of, 'oh it's so huge, I'm going to tell somebody about that.'"

❧

The cakes, the comfort food, and Sal's technique of going table to table and chatting with diners had earned The Café some good reviews. By 2005 it had expanded into the open space around its original 12 chairs to 150 chairs. Customers weren't any longer just antique browsers stopping for a bite. People were intentionally coming to the building just for lunch. The Café had become a destination.

But the uncertainty over whether The Café's lease would be renewed clouded the future. For a year Sal had asked the owners about the lease. It had expired in 2003 and now the Antique Mall agreement was month to month. Sal and Cindy would eventually learn that the Antique Mall was moving and that there would be space in the new location for The Café. By then, however, they had made other plans. The months of not knowing whether The Café would have a home drove home to Sal a lesson about the restaurant business that Cindy's father had learned decades earlier: it wasn't just about food, it was about real estate.

"We didn't have anything," says Sal. "We had a restaurant, but we didn't own the real estate. It all could have been evaporated by a simple, 'We're closing, and you don't have a lease.'"

Cindy still had the urge to just shut everything down and walk away from the stress of business ownership, but she recognized that would take the family farther from their goals of financial security. They talked to a consultant about selling the restaurant, but The Café was not a great asset an investor might want to buy. To get there you had to walk through a building and up the stairs. It was still relatively small, with a unique style of organizing the staff—there was no traditional owner-manager-employee hierarchy. Instead, workers were cross-trained in specific areas of the tiny kitchen—an employee would be in charge of production at the sandwich station, for example.

"They manage themselves," says Cindy. "They're not really managers, they're the leaders of their area. They take on the responsibility and make sure that it goes smoothly on their station, so collectively they're self-managing. They have a certain level of experience and set the tone and they have the respect of everybody else because they're working alongside them. They're not a manager who doesn't know how to do this stuff. They know how to do their job. And your job. It works out better for us."

But not for someone wanting a marketable asset. The consultant told them, "What you have here is so particular to you that you could never copy it," Cindy says. Sal remembers that differently. He says the consultant was offering an unpromising pay-up-front arrangement before he would work with them. Whichever version is true, Sal and Cindy needed to clear up The Café's cloudy future.

Sal says, "In my gut I knew if we stayed where we were that we would die and have nothing."

Sal saw a way forward. Cindy didn't like any of the choices they faced. She would say, "You want to do this all over again? Are you crazy?"

"I knew what it would take," she says. "Build a new kitchen. All the legal stuff. Getting all your licenses, dealing with the health department. It just goes on and on and on. I did not want to jump through those hoops again and try to recreate what we had over there."

Sal would counter.

"We put our blood, sweat, and tears into this. I hate to see it go away and have nothing. Right now we have nothing to sell but used equipment. If we shut it down and sold our equipment we'd barely cover our debts. We'd be right back where we started."

Sal had another reason to look for a different location.

"We had quite a bit of space, but people still thought of it as a little spot inside another building," Sal says. "Even though we had a few favorable reviews, the foodies and restaurant critics just saw us as this annexed part of the Antique Mall. I didn't feel that we'd be recognized as a legitimate restaurant in the community until we became independent."

Cindy reluctantly agreed that, oddly, the way out of owning a restaurant was to open a new restaurant.

"I said to Cindy, 'If we could find a new location and get it up and running, then we would have something to sell.'" Sal found what he believed was the perfect place.

Everyone else told him it was a terrible place.

એ

Two notable areas of Louisville are downtown, and four miles southeast of downtown, an area called the Highlands, a busy, walkable stretch of trendy restaurants, coffee shops, and offbeat stores like Electric Ladyland selling vintage records, posters, and paraphernalia, and Doo Wop Shop, with musical instruments. Just behind the commercial buildings lining the main drag of Bardstown Road lie the meandering streets of popular residential areas.

Among the neighborhoods in between those two prominent areas is a tough-to-find 48-acre enclave called Paristown, after an early settler who moved there from Paris, Kentucky, a small town in the middle of the state. In 2005, Paristown was bordered by buildings housing long-time wholesalers and contractors and in the shadow of grain silos once used by Pillsbury to make frozen biscuits. Five times a day, trains screeched and rumbled across a 1930s elevated bridge, almost right over an abandoned manufacturing building fronted by broken sidewalks. Sal looked at that building and saw a restaurant.

"I really tried to discourage him," says Realtor Marilyn Helvey, who at the time was a real estate partner and mentor to Sal. "The warehouse was just a shell. It was in such horrible condition. I said, 'It's a money pit.'"

Helvey wasn't the only one warning Sal. "My attorney had a lot more experience with restaurant real estate than I did, and he told me the same thing. I also heard it from my CPA.

"I knew there was risk. There's always risk. I just had an overwhelming feeling that the location was as good as bad," says Sal. "I felt it was a glass half full, not half empty. I felt that with the right decisions and right marketing, it was going to work."

Sal saw plenty of potential parking places. He saw a large, open room that could replicate the space at the Antique Mall, with room left over for things like a larger kitchen. Although it was tucked into an odd blend of buildings, it was just a few blocks from the intersection of two busy streets between downtown and the Highlands. He didn't pay enough attention to the fact that the building sat seven feet below the 100-year flood plain, an oversight that would cost him later.

Sal's initial attraction to the location came from his expertise in the restaurant and real estate businesses, and by doing his homework.

"I knew I wasn't going to be able to afford something on Bardstown Road. I needed a transitional location," he says. "To make real money in a restaurant you need a large enough space. The guideline is 150 seats, 5,000 square feet. At the price point we knew we were going to be working at, we could grow a business that could support a family and create the kind of income we were hoping to achieve."

The high-end Cherokee Triangle residential neighborhood seemed a million miles away, but Sal noticed it shared a zip code with Paristown—a zip code that ten years later would be one of the fastest-growing real estate areas in Louisville. Catty-cornered was the Louisville Stoneware building, which had been producing popular, sturdy pottery displaying distinctive patterns since 1815 and was owned by noted Louisville businesswoman, philanthropist, and activist Christy Brown.

"The fact that it was across the street from Louisville Stoneware was all I needed," says Sal. Brown had been a customer at The Café and even asked about locating a version of the restaurant in her building. Tour buses full of potential restaurant customers would regularly pull up along the narrow streets to tour the pottery plant. But Sal and Cindy looked around the tiny showroom and didn't see nearly enough space for a kitchen and dining room. As a neighbor, however, Sal figured a restaurant could do well by locating near "one of the longest-running businesses in Kentucky."

There was one more thing Sal needed. Money to make a move possible. A local bank had been talking to Sal about handling the money for The Café. No thanks, he said, we have a good financial relationship with our current bank. However…

"I told them we weren't interested in moving our accounts, but we were in the market to buy real estate," says Sal. "I didn't know if we could qualify, but lo and behold, we got it approved. It was a shock that we were able to buy that building, but they funded the purchase and the renovation to make it into a restaurant."

Another shock was on the way when Sal took Cindy inside.

"We went downtown to buy the new building and it was in one of those rooms in a bank where you just sign papers and I just signed my life away," says Cindy. "We had to go back to the Antique Mall, and since I hadn't really seen the new building because I'd been so busy working, I said, 'Let's stop by,' so when we went back to work I could either feel inspired or good about it. When I saw what it was we'd signed up for, I was crying. It was all ratty-looking, old broken-down industrial space. There were raccoons living in there. It had just rained and there were leaks. There was water on the floor along with oil spills on the concrete. And we're going to put a restaurant in here? We'll be trying to fix this up while we're working every day at a restaurant over there? I was so mad that Sal did this. I could have killed him."

The couple stood outside, looking at the huge garage doors, wondering how they would turn them into an entryway for a restaurant, when a Jaguar pulled up and Christy Brown jumped out, holding her miniature dog.

"Urban revitalization," she exclaimed.

"I'm thinking, 'what is she talking about?'" says Cindy. "'It doesn't look like anything's being revitalized here. It looks like crap.'"

But Brown had eaten with the lunch crowds at the Antique Mall and now she saw them coming to her part of town. Cindy says Christy

Brown "knew what we brought to the table. She knew the business we created at the Antique Mall. The wheels were turning in her mind."

Paristown *would* eventually go through a major upgrade. A brew pub would open up in the old grain silos, and a theater for live concerts would be built just up the street. But the Paristown transformation was years in the future, and invisible to Cindy and Sal. They had a restaurant to run. And another to build. And a real estate business to develop. And three children.

The renovation would take two years. The first year involved getting permits: a building permit, approval of architecture and engineering plans, change-of-use permission to rezone from a factory to a restaurant, leading up to a certificate of occupancy.

When work on the new building finally started, Sal and Cindy wanted the food, mood, and decor to help bring the current Antique Mall customers to the new location.

"We wanted continuity as much as possible," says Sal. "We tried to use the same bright colors, the rich reds, the yellows and greens."

And then there were those light fixtures the Antique Mall allowed The Café to hang above the tables.

"They became very popular," says Sal. "Over time the dealers were begging to get their lights at The Café because they got better visibility and would sell. So when we moved I bought all the lights in The Café, removed all the price tags, and hung them up in the new building."

When moving day finally came, it happened in a weekend, and an army from St. Paul church came to help.

"People at the church always felt they had a sense of ownership in The Café," says Tom Grieb, who at the time was senior pastor at St. Paul United Methodist. "We met early on a Saturday. I went with Sal to rent a truck and we loaded everything out. There were lots of people who pitched in. We had a kind of fire brigade moving the chairs down the stairs, then the tables, then all the other stuff. It was a long day. It was a fun day."

The Café's last day at the Antique Mall was Friday, October 26, 2007, and it reopened in Paristown by Tuesday. The new location brought mostly the same menu, but different ways of making that happen.

"It was basically starting over again," says Cindy. "The logistics were different. The kitchen setup was different. We had to hire more people because we had a kitchen that could put out a ton more food."

And, Cindy says, they wondered, "Will our Antique Mall customer base come to this area?"

The good news was that their customers did follow The Café to its new home. The bad news was that the economy was about to crash. The worldwide financial crisis of 2008 had actually started a couple years earlier with a collapse in the real estate market. In 2006, foreclosures in the U.S. rose 42 percent. In 2007, 75 percent, along with the biggest drop in home sales in almost 20 years. The plan for Sal's real estate business to replace the restaurant business was put on hold.

"In 2008 my real estate business just fell out of the sky. I was working on deals that never came to fruition. I went from $75,000 in 2006 to virtually nothing in 2007," he says.

"The Café was growing like gangbusters and Cindy needed me helping run the business at the new location," says Sal. "I put my real estate license in escrow and focused my entire energy on The Café."

Something else The Café brought from the Antique Mall as a way to keep their customer base was a price point—the restaurant term for what a diner expects to pay. For The Café, that was $10. Sal had calculated income and expense, but "projections are projections and when you set into reality, we weren't hitting our projections. We had to do something to generate more income."

They decided that something would be breakfast.

"We were really set up for lunch, we weren't a breakfast kitchen at all," says Cindy. "It's a whole other equipment package to set up for breakfast. Most people do breakfast on a long, stainless steel cooktop. But we couldn't afford anything new."

So Cindy reached back to her summer at Yellowstone National Park, where she learned to flip eggs to order in a pan. And, just as she learned by first flipping a piece of bread with a wrist flick, now she was teaching.

"I'd be there at 5:30 in the morning, and slowly but surely they all learned," she says. And just like Cindy nearly thirty years earlier, "We broke a lot of eggs."

Flipping eggs wasn't the only skill the refugee kitchen staff needed to learn.

"They didn't know what an American breakfast was," says Cindy. "They didn't know what scrambled eggs even looked like. The way Americans eat breakfast was a foreign concept to them."

And then there was grits.

"Even if you're American and you've never cooked grits, you think, this is the weirdest thing. How is this dry, hard thing going to turn into something edible?" she says. "I had to tell them no, it's not supposed to taste like that, it's supposed to taste fluffy, and try to get them to understand how grits could taste. But they had the desire to learn."

Cindy developed breakfasts that would be easy and quick to fix and still stand out as signature dishes. One was twice-baked French toast, soaked overnight, then baked so it could be fixed without the griddle they didn't have. Another was baked oatmeal.

"If we were going to have oatmeal, I wanted it to be a different experience. Not the goopy oatmeal being held in a steam well you could do at home. That doesn't represent something you go out for. I wanted it to be special. I thought we could do something in a casserole dish we could bake beforehand. We'd hold it cold then scoop it up, put fruit on it and heat it in the microwave. We could have them ready in a bowl, then all you do is put fruit on top of it, heat up a pitcher of milk, and it could be a different way to have something healthy."

While Cindy ran the kitchen, Sal managed the front, earning his reputation for visiting and chatting with each table, a reputation he carried from the Antique Mall. It was part of Sal's outgoing nature. It was also marketing.

"The owners of the Grisanti restaurants once told me customers would rather talk to a stupid owner than a smart manager," says Sal. "People like to say 'We're friends with the owner,'" he says, adding that his customer chats need to be genuine, and not just checking the box of visiting with diners. It's also customer satisfaction research. "If something is wrong, I really want to know. I want people to have a good experience."

As the crowds grew, especially at lunch, Sal refined another skill he had learned over the years: managing wait times. "It's a pretty basic equation," he says. "The restaurant has to be in the sweet spot, like 150 seats, about 40 tables. Once you have people waiting, you count the number of parties on the list, double that, then add five minutes. Invariably, it works perfectly."

Until it doesn't.

⁊

In the months after the move, The Café seemed biblically plagued. Five months after it opened, in March 2008, one of the nation's largest investment banks failed. The collapse of Bear Stearns started a year that brought on the recession that reached to every industry and around the world. US restaurants took a hit along with everything and everyone else. Bennigan's restaurants closed 150 locations in the United States and declared bankruptcy. By the end of the year the National Restaurant Association's monthly Restaurant Performance Index, which tracks the health and outlook of the US restaurant industry, fell to its lowest level since the measure started in 2002. That year's outlook still marks a historic low today.

"Everybody was just holding on for dear life," says Cindy. But The Café seemed well positioned to weather its first disaster, with that price point of under $10. So, Sal and Cindy doubled down. "We grabbed onto the mentality that we'll give them more. We would check other people's price points and we would cut back our price points. We'd beat them on price then give people more. They're not going to get this tiny little thing on their plate, they're going to get a great big thing on their plate and they'll go, 'Wow.'"

"The recession actually helped The Café," Sal says. "We started getting our reputation built up on the fact that we were a favorable choice when budgets were being slashed on business lunches."

Not every cloud came with such a silver lining, however.

A year after The Café opened at its Paristown site, Hurricane Ike made landfall off the Gulf of Mexico, spreading a windstorm across the middle of the country as far north as the Great Lakes. In Louisville, gusts as high as 80 miles per hour closed the airport and left 300,000 without power, the worst outage in 30 years. The Café survived the first round of the outage, but a week later, literally out of a clear blue sky, the restaurant's electricity went out for several days as the utility repaired a damaged substation nearby.

Four months later an even bigger power failure hit the city as part of a massive ice storm across the state. Temperatures stayed near 30 degrees for days, school closed for a week, and this time The Café didn't escape the loss of electricity and the resulting loss of income.

Seven months after that came the floods. The Café ended up paying a stiff price for Sal's lack of attention to the building's location below the flood plain. For hours on the morning of August 4, 2009, rainfall as heavy as more than eight inches an hour closed the interstates through town. Nearly 200 people were rescued from cars and buildings. Several feet of water stood around the University of Louisville campus, the main library branch, the Churchill Downs racetrack, downtown, and The Café. Sal and Cindy's restaurant required $30,000 of cleanup. Their flood insurance policy had a $50,000 deductible, leading to months of nerve-wracking negotiations with the IRS as Sal tried to prioritize how to pay bills.

∾

Sunday offered one bright spot during those turbulent times at the new location. While the Café earned about $2,500 a day during the week, the growing Sunday brunch crowd kicked that day's take up to about $3,000.

But son Clark saw a cost to that most profitable day of the week.

Clark grew up watching what long work hours and financial pressures could do to a family. Around the time Sal started looking for restaurant locations to replace the Antique Mall, Clark started talking to his parents about working too hard, about working seven days a week, about not taking off the Sabbath. Clark had traveled to China and South America for projects with different Christian groups, and he would help out at The Café during his trips back home. He made a point to take a Sabbath from work himself, and he wished his parents would take a weekly day off themselves. His reasons were both practical and faith-based.

"The Lord who designed us designed us not to be robots that keep going all the time," Clark says. "We are spiritual individuals that need time to ponder. If you don't organize your week to protect that time, you end up stealing it from other parts of your week, from your relationships with other people. Rest should be a habitual part of your week, not just to avoid burnout, but for your family and for being filled with love for God and his creation."

Clark's Sabbath was Wednesday. When he came home from his travels, the restaurant seemed least busy on Wednesday, and Wednesday was church meeting night. Clark says, "I needed that boundary and it was valuable."

Sal and Cindy's faith and spirituality had been a growing influence on their lives since they had joined St. Paul and been working to repair their marriage. Clark's Christianity seemed in a whole different league, however. If Clark's strictness about keeping his own Sabbath seemed unusual, extending that to the family business sounded risky to the income Sal and Cindy had been so desperately trying to preserve for the past ten years.

Clark was well aware of the importance of getting an income from the restaurant, so he made efforts to choose his words carefully, strategically. He researched and cited other successful faith-based restaurants. He asked his parents to close on Sunday and trust their business to God.

"I told them that I know you don't believe me," he says. "I know you've learned in your business classes and from your experience that this doesn't seem to pencil, but I'm telling you if you do it for the right reasons, not because you want to increase your sales but because you want to improve your spiritual life, improve your relationship with

PAUL WESSLUND

God and your fellow human beings, then you'll close on Sundays and you'll trust in the Lord for compensation."

That was a lot to swallow for a couple of restaurant owners trying to keep their business afloat. But Clark persisted.

"He would tell us at the end of the workday. He would tell us on our days off," says Cindy. "He would say, 'You really need to take care of yourselves. You need to take care of your staff. You need to give God the glory for what has happened here and out of that gratitude you will benefit way beyond what you could ever imagine.'

"I'd think, 'That's great theology, but in the real world, it doesn't work like that. How are we going to give up our busiest day?'"

On the other hand, she knew the effects of operating seven days on the family, and the staff.

"How are we going to keep people from quitting as more of them say, 'I want to be off on Sunday, I have this event at my church,'"? she says. "People would take Sunday off, and a Muslim woman who didn't have church on Sunday would feel pressured to work that day. Maybe we should be closed on Monday, give up our least busy day, but these women all wanted to be with their families on Sunday and so did we. We would have loved to have a Sunday of what it would feel like to go to church and then go home. It was huge."

Sal and Cindy started thinking, as Cindy puts it, "Clark can come up with some quirky things. But the more he kept nagging, the more it's like, maybe Clark's right."

Clark quit dropping hints and sat down with Sal one day at the restaurant for a direct conversation.

"I can visualize Clark and me sitting there and him telling me, 'Dad, you really need to honor the Sabbath. You and mom need time off. The only way you're going to get it is if you close one day a week.' I told him, 'I can't afford to close on Sunday,' and he would say, 'God would honor your decision. You just have to have faith.'

"I had it all laid out on a spreadsheet and we still had to fill the seats. I did not have the faith that God was just going to wave his hands and make it all good."

Then Mother's Day happened.

⁓

In the restaurant business, Mother's Day is Black Friday, a day of income that can make up for a lot of slow days. According to the National Restaurant Association, the top gift for Mom that day is a meal out with the family. Two out of five adults dine out on Mother's Day.

The first Mother's Day at The Café's new location was a relatively small affair. It was still building its business after having opened only about five months earlier, and breakfast had been on the menu less than four months. But by the next Mother's Day, 2009, The Café would be ready to put on a big show.

A special Mother's Day menu had been prepared to appeal especially to moms and to streamline production in the kitchen. It offered a couple of egg dishes, a couple of chicken salad items, a pasta salad, a peanut butter and jelly sandwich for the kids.

"When you're in the restaurant business you always try to figure out the best way to do Mother's Day," says Sal. "Some places do buffets, but we didn't think our menu lent itself to a buffet."

Sal's mathematical seating formula blew up. Cindy's kitchen collapsed.

"We were just onslaughted," says Sal. "It was the ugliest day ever."

The waiting line spilled out the door and around the block. The drug counselors Ron and Pat McKiernan and family waited in line outside, and even longer once they were seated.

"One of my clients was waiting tables there and he walked out and told me it's going to be a while, it's crazy," says Pat. Ron left angry, a legacy of the day that still haunts Sal. One of the servers quit on the spot in frustration.

"We had to pick up comp checks to the point we decided we can't be comping all these checks or we're going to lose our butts," says Sal. "We ended up letting some people pay in spite of the disaster."

Cindy calls it a "total fail. The kitchen crashed."

"We took too many reservations and we had people walking in and we put them on the books," she says. "We couldn't even execute the smaller menu because we had no practice. Our spirits were broken. Our kitchen was in disillusionment. This was a total fail and they knew how bad it was. We were supposed to do Mother's Day as a restaurant because it's the busiest day of the year. It's your best day. But not for us."

When the last customer left that day, Clark asked his mom what she wanted for her Mother's Day.

Across the river in Indiana there's a small family-favorite burger-and-ice-cream stand along a state road, called Polly's Freeze.

"It was a day of hell. I said, 'I just want to go to Polly's Freeze and sit outside, not in a restaurant. I don't want to be around servers and dishes, just go sit out on a picnic table and have a burger and ice cream,' and that's what we did. It was raining. We were all getting wet, but we didn't care. We were together."

It was The Café's best income day yet, bringing in $6,000, even with all the comped meals. But Cindy said, "Never again."

Clark says, "It was as if the Holy Spirit let it get so bad that they hadn't submitted their business to the Lord that he let them fall to the rock bottom when it came to their energy level and what it was doing to our family."

Sal says, "It was a financially great day, but it was so negative on our hearts, and that was more important to us than the cash. We decided that since something like 80 percent of our employees were mothers, we're like, 'What are we doing?'"

It was The Café's last Mother's Day, and Sal would spend the next 18 months figuring out how to close on Sundays while still earning enough money to stay open the rest of the week.

CHAPTER 11

The Hostess And Her Hats

Sal tells this story:

Victoria Petersen is special in my heart. The first time she applied I totally dismissed her as a non-candidate because she looked like a street person. A homeless waif. Skin and bones, basically. I could not see her as someone who worked at The Café. I didn't think she would represent us well.

But she was persistent and she came to apply on multiple occasions. I have a practice as a small business owner to always allow people to apply. I didn't keep her from applying, I just told her we didn't have anything for her.

One day she managed to clean herself up and I saw something in her, not the least of which was her persistence and her enthusiasm. I hired her as a busser, a position we call a service assistant that does the supportive roles to customer service. They're not generally customer contact but they have some customer interaction. They're not serving people; they run food and clean the tables. If they show promise, then they move up to things like greeting and seating guests. When I hired her, she was so excited she gave me a big hug and thanked me. She was affectionate but not inappropriately. You could tell she was expressive.

When I hired Victoria, we'd been open at the new location about three years, and I was the only host. I greeted every guest. I made all the decisions about where people were seated. Early on, we had others seating guests, but once the business got to the point where there was a wait, it required someone who knew what they were doing, who could quote realistic waiting times and coordinate reservations with walk-ins. It's a complicated process. When you go on a wait, the whole dynamic changes.

Victoria immediately blossomed. She engaged the customers. She was big on getting to know our regular customers, walking around the dining room, making them feel welcome and appreciated. For me that was huge. She would go out of her way to talk to a mother with her baby. She would pick the babies up and hold them and walk around so the mother could enjoy her meal. She was a bit unconventional in her approach. Some people didn't get that conduct. They thought she was a loose cannon—"What's she doing with that baby over there? It's a liability." I saw it as a pure spreading of joy and I celebrated it.

As I got to know her, she told me disturbing stories about being abandoned by her parents and being abused. She said that at sixteen she was basically out on the street. She became an exotic dancer and started using drugs and alcohol.

She got into recovery and was sober while she was working for us, but she also suffered from an eating disorder. She was so thin, customers and co-workers would express concern.

She was very stylish. She always wore hats. She had a closetful of hats and would wear a different one every day. She said it was to cover a scar on her forehead from getting hit with a bottle during a fight.

When she worked for us, we were open on Sundays, and she wanted to work all the time. She took very few days off. The Café was her happy place.

She'd been working for us for a little over a year when we decided to close for a week. It was July, and we always close around July fourth. She begged us not to close. She said she needed The Café. I dismissed it. I said, "You'll be fine. There's plenty of other things you can do."

She relapsed while we were closed. When we reopened, she was on the street and using again. She wanted to come back to work, but she couldn't. She needed to go into treatment. She checked herself in to the detox center, but at that point I didn't understand how things worked. It's all voluntary, so if you don't want to stay, they just let you go. They can't hold you.

She got into a 30-day program at another treatment center where she had a room and a time to go into groups. When she was in one of those groups she slumped over, her heart gave out, and she died. EMS was called, but it was too late. I remember exactly where I was when I got the call, in the basement at our house, and I totally broke down. I felt really responsible. Since then we've tried to restructure how we take our vacations, and to hire people to run things while we're gone.

My reaction was one of guilt. I wasn't there for Victoria. I didn't see this coming. I think it propelled me to become deeper, more deliberately involved in helping people. I'm more intimately involved in asking questions and holding people accountable.

❧

Sandra Harris is a retired educator in Louisville, still working part time and making jewelry and framing art. She's married to Phil Wood and has one son, Bryan Harris. Sandra tells this story:

Victoria called me "Mama." I met her through a friend when she was in her early twenties. She was in recovery, she'd been sober a few months, and she was working with a sponsor. She had never gotten a driver's license, so I gave her rides to her AA meetings and to work.

She and her three siblings were taken from their parents when she was seven. She was the oldest and was like the mother hen for her brother and two sisters. When they appeared on Wednesday's Child (a television segment for a foster-parent recruitment program), Victoria was the one who grabbed the mic and started singing. She loved to be the center of attention. She was ten or twelve. All four of them were adopted, but it didn't work out well for Victoria. She got started on methamphetamine and alcohol. I think she was struggling to fit in at school. She had an eating disorder and started bingeing and purging in addition to her addiction to meth and alcohol.

She went to a recovery center, then a home for girls, where she ran off with one of the counselors. She and the counselor and her sister and brother all lived together in this little apartment, and Victoria was taking care of everybody, working as a table dancer. When the relationship with her counselor didn't work out, she left and went from house to house. People would take her in, usually guys, because she was cute and very charming. She reminded me of Tinker Bell. She gave off this light, and all she wanted to do was love people. She gave hugs, grabbing me so tightly I could hardly breathe. Nobody's ever hugged me like Victoria.

One night I picked her up to take her to one of her meetings and she told me she was living with a man who had taken pity on her and had taken her under his wing, but he wanted more in the relationship and she wasn't comfortable with that. He was nice and he was respectful of her, but she didn't know how to get out. I suggested she look for a job and look for an apartment. She mentioned that she never really felt like she had a mother. She asked me if I had a daughter and I said, "No, but I've always wanted a daughter." She called me Mama ever since.

She eventually got an apartment downtown in subsidized housing.

One of the places I suggested she could work was The Café because I knew other women Sal had hired. After she didn't get hired, I took her shopping and bought her clothes. She called me and told me she had gotten a job at The Café.

She texted me every morning so I could see what she was wearing and how cute she looked. She told me she loved me every time I saw or talked to her. She gave me the gift of having the best mother-daughter relationship for three and a half years that anyone could ever have. She was sober almost all of that time.

Victoria loved hats. She wore a hat every day at work. Sal said, "You look good in hats; it's a great brand having my hostess in a hat." He only had to say it once. She had a scar from being cut on the forehead with a beer bottle in a fight during her drinking days. It wasn't that bad, but she liked that her hats covered up the scar. But she did look good in hats.

She was so charming, but she struggled with appropriate behavior. I was at The Café for lunch one winter day when a couple came in and one of the men wore a long fur coat and a fur hat. Twenty minutes later she comes over to my table wearing his hat, saying, "Look what he gave me." I told her to give it back, you don't take things from your customers. She looked at me like she was going to kill me.

Everybody wanted to take her home and to take care of her. I wanted her to be independent. I wanted her to get her GED. I wanted her to grow up.

At the school where I worked, one of the drug education classes had troubled students who might benefit from Victoria's experience. She had been in art therapy, she was very talented and artistic, and when I asked if she would meet with the class she said she'd love it. She brought a sample of her art to share with them. She said, "Instead of talking to them at their desks, why don't we all sit around the table and I'll give them paper and get them started drawing?" She talked to them about how she had ruined her teeth doing meth and she took out her false teeth and showed them. She talked about what life was like using drugs and how it was better not using drugs. The kids ate her up. I think for the first time she was a legitimate role model to some kids that needed somebody with credibility and some depth and weight in her message. As she talked with them, they were sharing with her and drawing their own expressions on paper with her guidance.

She had an eating disorder her whole life, but I didn't even know it until one time my husband came in from the back yard where he had seen she threw up dinner. I confronted her about it and started taking her to a nutritionist. After a couple months, she said, "Don't spend your money on that any more; I'm not getting anything out of it." I took her to a doctor and he said her potassium was so low he didn't understand how she was up and walking around. I said, "Victoria, you need to tell him why." She was so mad at me. The doctor told Victoria she needed to go to the hospital and she said she wouldn't. I told her it was a serious condition, and she said, "I'm old enough to say no, and I'm not going to miss work." I tell myself I should have tried harder, I should have threatened her or something, but she was very stubborn.

People came to The Café to see Victoria. She lit up the room. The fact that people came to see her gave her a reason to be at work and gave her an opportunity to give joy back to them.

Two weeks before she died, her recovery sponsor called me. Victoria had started drinking again, and her sponsor was taking her to detox. Later I picked her up from there and took her to a treatment center. One weekend I was at a school retreat out of town. When I came into my room from a session, I saw I had four calls from the treatment center and at least that many from the hospital. I knew something was wrong. This was Sunday, August 1, 2010.

She had been palling around with everybody at the treatment center, playing air guitar and singing "Hound Dog," which was so typical of her. She sat down in a chair to rest and everybody thought she was taking a nap. Her heart just stopped beating. I asked the medical examiner to do a toxicology report. I don't think she was using at the time. He said her body just wore out. She was twenty-seven years old. She always looked younger than her age, but health-wise she was much older.

To Victoria, The Café meant family. The people who came and loved her and ate there because they liked seeing her validated her very existence. She was a forgiving person. It pained her when people mistreated her, and she wanted to turn that around and show them love. Her sponsor called her an angel of love. I called her a light. She's still a light.

Victoria's story is about a human being who had a rough start and had to learn how to love pretty much on her own and did it masterfully. She and The Café are inextricably connected. It was like a home to her. I'm grateful to Sal for hiring her and seeing what she could be, because those were the last three years of her life and she was happy.

CHAPTER 12

Far From Home

Burmese Pumpkin Chicken Stew
Makes 6 servings

1 small Hokkaido pumpkin, 6 inches in diameter (or butternut or delicata squash)

3 boneless, skinless chicken breasts

1 large white onion

1 head garlic

1 piece fresh ginger root, 2 inches long

1/2 cup vegetable oil

1 tsp salt

1 tsp paprika

1/2 tsp black pepper

1 Tbsp powdered or granulated chicken stock, or Better Than Bouillon base

1 bunch fresh cilantro

Scrape out the seeds from the pumpkin or squash. You may peel the pumpkin or delicata squash, or leave the rind on; they will both get soft enough to eat. But the butternut squash should be peeled. Dice pumpkin into chunks 1 to 2 inches long. Set aside.

Dice chicken into cubes 1 inch thick. Set aside.

Dice onion, garlic, and ginger into a fine mince. Set aside.

Sauté onion, garlic, and ginger in vegetable oil in soup pot over moderate heat until vegetables begin to brown. Add chicken and sauté until meat begins to brown. Add pumpkin, salt, paprika, black pepper, and chicken stock. Simmer, covered, until pumpkin is tender and chicken is cooked, about 30 minutes.

Serve sprinkled with freshly chopped cilantro leaves. Serve over rice or lentils.

S hit."

Sal was taking inventory at The Café and trying to move containers around.

"Shit. Shit."

One of the cooks in the kitchen turned to him. She was a Muslim refugee who had worked there for years.

"Don't say 'shit, shit,'" she told Sal. "Say, 'Thank you, God.'"

"She really humbled me," says Sal. "You think about yourself as a Christian and trying to lead by example, and then someone unexpected teaches you about faith and how to walk the walk."

For her part, when this relatively new American citizen tells her version of that story about Sal, she says, "I think he now gets it. In the morning when you wake up, say 'Thank you, God, I woke up today.' You have what you need. You have family, you have a house, you have food every day. Too many people do not have a house, do not have food. After you eat, you need to say, 'Thank you, God.'"

I won't identify this kitchen worker in The Café any further. She fled persecution along with some of her family—others remain overseas, and with today's strong and complicated views and politics about refugees all over the world, who knows what could frustrate her hopes of the rest of her family rejoining her. She misses them.

She came to the United States and The Café with more than a faith lesson for Sal. She grew up learning skills and love for cooking. She especially taught Cindy about baking.

"She saw me struggling with this recipe for sweet potato cinnamon rolls," says Cindy. "I'm not a huge yeast baker, and she said, 'Let me try.' She made that yeast grow like no other, she knew exactly what kind of cloth to use and put it over this big bowl and put it in a warm spot. She knew how to work it. For years she was the only person who could make the yeast bread."

The Kentucky Refugee Ministry's John Koehlinger sees The Café as helping refugees transition to a place where they don't know the language or customs by offering women a job more suited to their backgrounds than work at a meat-packing plant or other manual labor.

"Not all of them would have been easily employed elsewhere," he says. "Working in a kitchen preparing food and serving food is something that connects with who they are."

Cindy says, "They cooked for the village or they just enjoyed cooking because that was pretty much their job, to provide food for their family, and they were very resourceful."

The Café offers refugees two more abstract employment benefits particularly valuable to them: trust and relationships.

"They're looking for a social interaction at their workplace, a camaraderie," says Cindy. Her mantra of "I wanted them to see we were who we said we were" provided another basic job benefit.

"They didn't know in their country that you could trust or count on somebody," says Cindy. "They knew every day that we'd do what we said we were going to do. That spoke volumes to them."

Sal and Cindy took an interest in their lives and their families.

"We wanted to know about their country. We wanted to know about their foods. We were curious," says Cindy. That attention translated into trust. "They feel safe. There's not anybody out to get them. Not anybody sabotaging them. It's a safe place."

The woman who called out Sal's cursing says, "You can talk about any problem with Sal. He understands."

Cindy cites benefits beyond a day's work that The Café has received from the refugees, especially during the darkest days of the business.

"I didn't always want to come into work the next day, so it was truly inspirational to me how they were working really hard to survive," she says. "They were not giving up on me. There was a lesson in humility there every day. They were pushing every day to have a better life. So together we could do it again. They're tough because they just had to survive under conditions I can't even begin to understand. They figure out how to do it faster, more efficiently."

Koehlinger says, "Refugees are survivors. They don't take that job with Sal and Cindy for granted. It's the first paycheck they've had in a very long time. It's the American Dream. It's still available."

For Cindy, "The way they would impact me through their culture, through their stories, through their families, through their faith, whether it be Hindu, Buddhist, Muslim, it didn't matter. They impacted me because I saw the same meaning of love played out again and again. Compassion, love, it didn't matter where it came from, or what culture. It was the same."

The refugee who schooled Sal on cursing taught a different lesson to Cindy—a lesson as small as a kitchen gadget and as big as faith in the ability to work through life's problems.

It was time to make soup in the kitchen, calling for eight large cans of crushed tomatoes. But the crank on the can opener wasn't working.

Cindy fretted, "How are we going to do that?"

Cindy's co-worker, the expert with yeast who preached saying thank-you to God for waking up in the morning, grabbed a butcher knife and, holding it up and down, set the point at the edge of the rim of a can. She whacked the handle with the palm of her hand so that it punctured the edge of the lid and slid inside. She then worked the blade around the edge until the lid came off. "I never had a can opener," she said.

"They've had to solve so many everyday problems in their lives, not having what they needed," says Cindy. "They brought all that resourcefulness to our kitchen and taught me, don't worry, it's going to be OK even though that's not working. We're going to do this."

✧

Sitting in the rain at the Polly's Freeze hamburger stand after the disastrous Mother's Day, the family agreed: no more Mother's Days at The Café.

"We wanted to celebrate our mother on Mother's Day," says Clark. "We didn't want to see her working her fingers to the bone. That was the worst part, seeing our own mother bending over backwards for other mothers, and I think our father could see that in our eyes."

Clark saw the trauma as another symptom of running a business seven days a week. So he took the moment as an opportunity, and tried yet again to get his parents to take Sunday off, this time with a new twist to his argument.

"I said something like, 'Dad, if you're closed one day a week and it happened to be on Sundays, then you wouldn't have to explain why you're closed on Mother's Day.'"

One year later The Café did have to tell some customers that while it was open Sundays, Mother's Day was not one of them. Even though they closed that one Sunday, Sal was not ready to kill the golden goose that was Sunday brunch.

"I'm not one to do knee-jerk reactions," says Sal. "I process and analyze."

Cindy had another reason to close on Sunday.

"Cindy would say, 'I'm tired of things happening to us. I want us to get control of the situation,'" says Sal. "Closing on Sunday was something that we could control, get some order in our lives. Let's have one day a week where we can decompress, be a family, and become more faithful servants of Christ."

Cindy's view from the kitchen offered still another perspective.

"Getting the gangbuster business on Sundays after church worked almost too well some days," she says. "We would have days where huge numbers of people would sit down all at once in the dining room when a couple of churches would let out. There would be large groups, tens, twelves, eights, people leaving church and saying, 'Let's go get brunch.' The kitchen would crash because we just couldn't get the food out quick enough."

Sal kept looking for an answer.

"I wanted to be certain," he says. "I wasn't just going to close on Sunday and not have a plan for how we were going to replace those sales."

Sal's spreadsheets showed what he was up against. The Café had just started breaking even by bringing in $2,500 a day Monday through Saturday, and $3,000 on a typical Sunday. The arithmetic showed that closing on Sunday would mean somehow, The Café would need to boost sales $500 a day the six days it would be open.

Sal faced another problem.

"I was getting pushback from a lot of the service staff." They ran their own numbers, he says. "I said I'm thinking about closing on Sunday and they said, 'What, are you crazy? I make more money in tips on Sunday than the whole rest of the week.' Thinking about the impact on my staff was as difficult as anything. When you remove a day, that's ten shifts. It's like two people. Some people were going to lose their jobs or go from full time to part time."

Yet another concern: how would all those loyal brunch customers react?

Then a customer suggested an elegantly simple idea. Open an hour earlier and close an hour later.

The Café's hours ran from 8:00 to 3:00. The customer said 8:00 was too late for a breakfast business meeting, but he'd come at 7:00. Today Sal jokes that customer never did come in at 7:00, but the idea sent Sal back to his spreadsheets. He sliced and diced the numbers, combing through them to find that $500 extra a day. He cut that income requirement into two parts, $250 in the extra morning hour and $250 in the afternoon—at $15 a head that's about 30 more breakfasts, 30 more late-afternoon people, and about 10 more at noon. With numbers like those, The Café would be able to replace the lost business from closing on Sundays.

Another bit of arithmetic stared back at him that made a decision to close on Sundays even easier: Sunday hours were 10:00 to 3:00. All the income generated on Sunday happened in just five hours. The new extended hours during the week would come to twelve hours. By closing on Sunday, The Café would actually be operating seven more hours a week.

"Two more hours each of the other days would mean adding twelve hours a week, which is more hours than we're open on Sunday," he reasoned. "They're not prime hours but they're still operational hours. People are cognizant of your hours so whatever those hours are, they don't start coming right when you open and there aren't many around when you close. So we don't see many more customers between 7 and 8 or 3 and 4, but we see far more than we did before between 8 and 3.

It just increased the overall volume."

Sal knew different hours wouldn't magically bring in customers, and he knew The Café had built its reputation on lunches. In fact the restaurant was already at capacity from 11:30 to 1:30. Sal arranged for a segment on a popular radio show where the DJ would talk about breakfast at The Café.

"We got some new customers from that and even had people come in and say, 'You mean you serve lunch, too?'"

Catering added yet another positive column to the balance sheet.

"We took a look at our production capability," says Sal. "We've got these people, they're on staff, they're on the clock, and between 11:30 and 1:30 we max out our production capability. But between 7 and 11:30 and 1:30 and 4 it's tapered out. That's when we can produce the box lunches and sandwich trays for corporate meetings. Those people want their lunches delivered at 11 o'clock. That's perfect for us because the staff can work on those from 9 to 11 then a delivery person takes it out the door and those people turn to making lunch for the dining room. That's called productivity."

Sal says, "It didn't take us long to get to that $3,000 a day, which immediately replaced the money lost on Sunday. With catering we can even get up to $5,000 a day."

Even the brunch crowd accommodated the change.

"There was an initial pushback from customers saying, 'Where are we going to go after church?'" says Sal. "But we transitioned over to Saturday. People who wanted to come to The Café for brunch would come on Saturday. So Saturday developed into a big day for us, which before was marginal at best.

"It was a leap of faith. But I felt like the numbers were reasonable, and we blew those numbers out of the water. We were validated fairly quickly."

Looking back on the long decision-making process it took to finally close on Sundays, Sal laughs as though acknowledging he might have been ignoring repeated divine instructions. "We were like, smitten" with wind storm, ice storm, and flood, he says. But his admitted "paralysis by analysis" has at least one defender—his minister at the time.

"We have that inward sense where you seek what God might be saying, but there's a period of discernment," says Tom Grieb. "We'll call that year and a half a time of discernment. There's practicality involved, but against the backdrop of a strong, faithful response. Discernment takes time. It takes us to a place where we can get at least some resolve, if not peace. At the end of discernment, we still have to take a leap of faith."

And though the servers in the dining room had been concerned about losing their Sunday brunch tip money, Cindy found immediate support for the decision among the kitchen staff.

"We came into the kitchen one day and said, 'We're going to be closed on Sunday,' and they were throwing their hands up, saying, 'Oh my gosh, thank you, we can stay home with our families.' It was evident right away it was the right thing to do, even though we didn't know if we could stand the loss of income," says Cindy. "They were thankful they would now have a day to regroup and be home with their children, on a day when they were home from school. They could go to wherever they worshiped. We had all different faith communities. We had the Muslim community, the Hindu community, the Buddhist community, the Christian community. We hired from all these ethnic groups representing all different types of people, and they all recognized what it meant to be off on that day."

❧

Several of the employees celebrating the Sunday closing had come to The Café in a fever of hiring as Sal tried to staff The Café's new location. When Kentucky Refugee Ministries brought a group of candidates from camps in Thailand, Sal says, "I was only going to hire two of them, and then I said, 'We'll just hire all of them. We'll figure out where we're going to put them.'"

They spoke no English. Their life experience was from villages surrounded by the southeast Asian jungles in Burma, and in refugee camps in neighboring Thailand. The everyday customs and knowledge of surviving in a mid-size American city were new to them. So was the culture of starting an 8-hour workday at exactly the same time every day. Before being taken from the refugee camp to the Bangkok airport for the long flight to the United States, some had never ridden in a motorized vehicle.

They were part of a group of people called the Karen, pronounced kuh-REN, that has been part of a civil war in Burma for more than 60 years. Or longer by some accounts. The Karen are the largest minority ethnic group in Burma, and their history goes back more than 2,000 years, when they moved from Mongolia to what is now the area around the Thai-Burma border. Conflicts in the region since then arise especially from World War II, when the Karen fought alongside the British with a promise of independence that never happened. In the following decades several groups protested and fought for democracy and for independence from Burma. Even the name of the country is a flashpoint, with an official change in 1989 to *Myanmar* that many see as illegitimate.

For the Karen people it added up to having to flee their villages from attacks by the Burmese army—attacks with widely reported atrocities that included burning villages to the ground, murder and rape, and using people as human mine detectors. In the 1980s so many Karen moved across the border into northern Thailand that refugee camps were set up. Today there are nine camps along the border with about 86,000 refugees.

Steve Clark and Annette Ellard have spent years getting to know Karen people. They're a married couple living in Louisville and working as field personnel for the Cooperative Baptist Fellowship, a network of churches, individuals, and global missions. Their first meeting with Karen people in 2001 was not with refugees, but to help paint a building in Thailand where students could come in from mountain villages to continue school beyond the sixth grade.

A new direction for their lives evolved as the refugee camps in Thailand grew. By 2006 more than 100,000 Karen living in those camps were identified as "a population of special humanitarian concern to the United States due to the persecution they have experienced," according to a US State Department news release at the time. In 2006 and 2007 more than 12,000 Karen refugees resettled into several U.S. cities, including Louisville. The communities got ready.

"A lot of refugee agencies across the country were prepared with Burmese-speaking interpreters," says Annette. One problem: "They do not speak Burmese, never mind the fact that the Karen considered the Burmese their enemy."

The large numbers of people new to the habits of American society overwhelmed the preparations. Steve and Annette's trips to Thailand suddenly made them valuable resources.

"In Thailand we were sleeping in their homes, eating their food, and traveling through their countryside, so we were learning a lot," says Steve.

Annette says, "We didn't have a broad, deep knowledge, but we had the relationship with the Karen people, so we at least had a starting point. We started learning everything we could."

They used that knowledge and those relationships to bring two societies together.

"We had no idea of the scale of what was coming. We thought it was going to be a few families. We didn't know it was this mass thing," says Annette. "The language problem and the lack of cultural interpretation were devastating. Steve and I found ourselves having meetings with social service agencies, with schools, with churches, and with employers."

Steve says, "We were trying to help them understand the folks they were hiring or servicing so they would be better able to understand how to deal with them.

"Folks that are coming out of Burma, they're rice farmers and they hunt for their meat and they get vegetables that they grow or that grow wild in the forest. They come here and they're thrown into systems they don't understand."

One huge cultural difference, says Steve, is as basic as time.

"For us, everything is linear. Things go on a timeline. But for them, it's a spider web. They don't tell things in chronological sequences. When you ask somebody to tell you how they got to this country, they'll tell you a few different things that don't help you figure out their story. That's tricky when their kids are going to school or learning history."

Time runs differently in a refugee camp, where employment is not allowed because the settlement is supposed to be a temporary solution—even though many of them have existed for more than 30 years.

And even if someone learns to get to a job on time, that's just the beginning of understanding our sophisticated sense of schedules.

Annette describes a Karen refugee woman, "a widow with children, a baby that was born right before coming to the U.S. She got the don't-be-late-for-work thing, but she was overwhelmed by trying to manage that with her children and the school schedule and the bus schedule and how to navigate so that she could meet this most important of all American goals, to be on time."

One day Annette went to a high school orientation to help Karen refugees learn the ropes of the public school system, and that's where she met Cindy Rubino, who was there with one of The Café's Karen employees.

"Sal and Cindy were investing in the lives of the people who worked for them," says Annette. Steve adds, "They're not just paying and supervising them. What makes The Café so different is Sal and Cindy see it as a relationship, not just a job. It's a different attitude. Their Christianity and their personalities play more of a role than just operating a business."

In 2007 Steve and Annette made another trip to Thailand, this time to visit the refugee camps to get a better idea of the background of the Karen they were working with. They visited two camps. One, Tham Hin, had been established ten years earlier, with an emphasis on being a temporary settlement. Part of making it temporary meant requiring houses to be no more than three feet apart, and instead of traditional roofs made of dried leaves, they had to be black plastic sheeting—which Steve says turned them into toaster ovens in the tropical climate. Houses tended to be dirt-floor, two-story wood or bamboo structures, the ground floor serving as an open-to-the-outside wood-fired kitchen, the upper level for sleeping. People ate on outdoor benches along the dirt roads where children played. Clothes were washed and scrubbed outside in plastic tubs. Some of the classrooms were supplied with desktop computers with UNHCR stickers—United Nations High Commission for Refugees. When refugees arrived, they would register, allowing them a UN food distribution. Ten thousand people lived in the 28-acre area.

The other camp they visited, Mae La, was larger and more established, having started in 1984, and was not as densely populated. In

2007 about 35,000 lived there on about 450 acres, though that population has grown to about 50,000 as of 2019. There was more room for gardening, and no requirement for black plastic roofs. Steve and Annette say it looked more like a traditional Karen village. A Bible school there offered seminary graduate-level education that attracted people from outside the camp.

Annette and Steve ventured across the river into Burma to visit a village called an IDP, for Internally Displaced People, who had fled after attacks on another village. Only later were they told the trails they took while in Burma were surrounded by mines. Within three years after their visit, the IDP village was attacked and burned, sending 4,000 people across the river into Thailand.

Among the gatherings at the refugee camps are briefings about applying for programs to settle in another country. Annette says that decision is not as easy as she first thought.

"We're very proud of our country and what we have as Americans. We think, why wouldn't other people want it? I learned people really wanted to go home. But they couldn't. Given that they couldn't go home and have the life they wanted in their homeland, having a chance to start a new life in a free country they saw as a great opportunity. But having to tear themselves away from everything they had ever known was something I hadn't given appropriate thoughtfulness to, the idea of leaving everything and hoping for something good."

When resettlement starts, a process of paperwork and vetting that can take three years, it ends with a 24-hour notice to pack all the family belongings in bags. And when they arrive in their new country, Steve says one refugee told him they are like babies—without knowing the local language, they can't talk; they don't know how to get places, so they can't walk; they don't have a way to get out and shop, so they can't feed themselves. "What we need are good American parents," he told Steve.

Steve and Annette learned refugees are not just strangers in a strange land. It also matters how they got here. Being driven from their homes by the horrors of war, adjusting to the life in a refugee camp, then resettling their family again into an entirely foreign culture, all take tolls.

"Every refugee that comes to the United States has some form of PTSD (Post Traumatic Stress Syndrome) just from what has created their refugee situation," says Steve.

Annette adds, "I learned I don't need to figure out whether they have PTSD, I need to figure out how severe it is and how they can learn to cope and navigate."

As the Karen looked for communities to orient themselves to Louisville, many joined Crescent Hill Baptist Church.

Crescent Hill Baptist's pastor Jason Crosby will tell you that connection started more than 200 years ago when Baptist missionaries first visited Burma in the 1800s. Today, while most Karen are Buddhist, of the 20 percent or so who are Christian, most are Baptists.

In early 2007, Steve and Annette were making plans for the Karen arrivals. As a first step, they contacted an interpreter and invited her to their church, Crescent Hill Baptist. Three days later they met with their first Karen refugees, who asked the interpreter where she went to church.

The answer to that question sent Steve and Annette's life, and the life of Crescent Hill Baptist Church, in new directions.

The Karen family told other refugees about the church they were about to visit, and by the next Sunday, Steve and Annette brought 19 Karen to church from four families.

"It snowballed," says Annette. "By Easter there were 53 Karen people at Crescent Hill Baptist Church. It was a hundred something by July." Annette says even some Buddhists were coming to Crescent Hill Baptist in search of a familiar Karen community.

As Jason Crosby spent time with the Karen in the congregation, he would hear about The Café. He officiated at a Karen wedding for a woman who met her husband while she was working at The Café. Sal was one of the men who walked her down the aisle.

"Eventually I put the pieces together," says Crosby. "I saw what the Rubinos were doing. Sal and Cindy made it a great point to know what was going on in people's lives."

Steve and Annette see The Café as a place that's about relationships. From walking around and chatting with diners, to getting involved in the lives of their employees—lending money for a child's school pizza party or joining them for a traditional Karen meal in their homes.

"I know their customers feel that The Café is their place," says Annette. "And that's how it is for the employees. They feel like they belong there and have a relationship that goes beyond punching your time card, doing your job, then going home."

As The Café's Karen employees were adjusting to their new lives, Sal and Cindy's son Clark was visiting between his international trips with Christian groups. He had just returned from South America and was getting ready for another trip to China. As an English teacher in China, he told his parents, he was part of what he calls "English corners"—small, informal groups that meet to discuss everyday uses of a new language. Cindy thought Clark's English corners could help the refugees at The Café.

"I remember my mom saying, 'That's what our staff needs,'" says Clark. "They want to communicate with us. They want to communicate with others. They want to make friends. Their kids need help with their homework.

"It was a free talk, a free chat, where they could get their thoughts together and ask questions about what they were interested in. My mom and maybe some others participated; they would give us phrases and ask, 'How do I answer this question? Is that the right way to say it?' And we could say, 'Yes, that's the right way', or 'If you say it this way, it sounds better.'"

There was only time for a handful of English circles with the Karen kitchen workers because Clark was traveling in and out of the country during those years. And sometimes the English circles that were held were delayed.

"I'd say, 'Let's start the English corner at four thirty,' when most of the customers had left, but my mom would say to me, 'They have to go get their kids at school at four.'"

So when everyone returned from picking up children at school, the English corner might turn into a homework session.

"The kids would get out their homework and we would give them some confidence building, to say, yeah, you're doing it well, so they can feel like they're not alone with doing their homework," says Clark. "One of the older mothers said her children's homework was so hard she couldn't understand it. She would ask if it was right. I would check it and say, yes, she's going to do well. They were worried their kids weren't completing their homework, and they just needed a little bit more confirmation to settle their anxiety."

Life interfered in other ways with the English circles for the Karen employees.

"Sometimes my mom would be the one shuttling people back and forth, especially on snowy days when the weather was bad. She didn't want their kids standing at the city bus stop, so she would drive them home."

Clark spent more time getting to know the Karen workers, while he helped out as a server or assistant manager at The Café, by joining them on their lunch breaks.

"I'd help them practice their English and have casual conversations with them, laugh and tell jokes," he says. And he watched the dynamics among the Rubinos, the Karen families, and the work of The Café. In the age before smartphones, he saw his dad using the office computer to download and print out maps and directions to help his employees navigate the city.

"My parents were like mentors to many of their staff," says Clark. "They would help with a letter of recommendation or giving resources for homework. The refugees got Sundays off, they got a community, they got a safe work environment—my parents would not tolerate any form of bigotry from their staff."

In return, says Clark, his parents "saw they were getting value from these hard workers who were willing to listen, who were willing to grow with the company and to learn. They wanted to keep them, so they began to think about, well, what are their struggles? What would be the things that would keep them from being able to do this job? There's other jobs that pay a similar amount. How can we control our costs and still pay them a salary that is competitive? We can give them other things that they need, help them in their lives. It's a combination of their moral obligation, their ethics, and it made good business sense." Clark remembers helping one of the Karen women in particular get to her GED class on time. She invited Sal and Cindy to a traditional dinner at the family home. She's the woman whose wedding Sal walked in at Crescent Hill Baptist. She says Sal is like her godfather. After losing family members during the fighting in Burma, then spending sixteen years in a Thai refugee camp where she was raising two children, she applied for resettlement in America.

"Learning English was very difficult for me," she says. "I'm still learning."

One of the goals in learning English was to pass the US citizenship test, which she did. Sal and Cindy attended the naturalization ceremony in a large downtown theater, where she became an American.

"The citizenship test is very hard," she says. "You have to learn about the history of the government. You study about freedom of speech. You need to know about all of American history. I learned you've got to follow the law. If you do, no problem. I'm proud of myself. I'm an American citizen now. Here you're not worried about fighting. You don't worry about what will happen tomorrow."

She brought to her job at The Café cooking skills she learned growing up and then raising her own family, as well as ingenuity. When a plumber quoted $3,000 for a new sewer line to her Louisville house, she went to the store, bought the piping, and she and her husband installed it themselves.

As she watches her children move through school and toward careers, she also wants them to remember their traditions.

"I don't want them to forget our culture. It's important to remember where we come from," she says. Instead of cooking a turkey for Thanksgiving, she makes a Burmese pumpkin chicken stew.

"I have a garden outside the house. I grow pumpkin, cilantro, basil. I have lemongrass. At home I cook rice, noodles, everyday Asian food. I taught my kids to cook. My youngest son is very picky. He goes to other people's houses to eat and he comes back and says, 'It has no flavor, Mom.'"

❧

As much as refugees value their lives in the United States, Annette says, "By and large this is not where they really want to be. It's their second choice. They want to be home with the people they know and in the culture they know."

Even finally landing a job in their new country can add to the weight of all the decisions that took the refugees farther from their homeland with each step.

"The trauma continues after they put their feet on American soil," says Annette. "It doesn't take them long to figure out they're providing cheap labor in jobs that Americans don't want to do, and that can be a very painful thing."

"Sal and Cindy have a very different model at The Café," says Annette. "They're in a relationship with their employees as individuals. When people can go to work in a place where not only are they not discriminated against, but they're loved, that's life-changing."

Steve describes how that business model has given The Café a stable workforce.

"People in the Karen culture tend to be community-oriented, family-oriented, and they're loyal. They will attach themselves to people like Sal and Cindy who treated them like family."

I asked Steve what people should know about refugees.

"They're really families dying for inclusion," he said. "If somebody notices them, pays attention to them, welcomes them, holy mackerel, that makes all the difference. That's the thing that refugees need the most, just being seen."

CHAPTER 13

Addiction, Recovery, and Compassion in the Workplace

Dorito Casserole
Serves 3-6

1 lb. ground beef

2 (10.5-oz) cans Campbell's tomato soup

2 (4-oz) cans diced green chilis, mild

1 large bag (9 3/4 oz.) Nacho Cheese Doritos

1 medium bag (2 cups) shredded mild cheddar cheese

Brown hamburger, drain. Add tomato soup, chilis, stir until mixture thickens.
Lay Doritos in casserole dish (may not need to use the whole bag.) Pour mixture
over chips. Cover with shredded cheese. Bake at 350 degrees for 20–30 minutes
until cheese is brown.

J eff taps the face of his phone.
"Four hundred seventy-five days I have today," he says. "I don't
even keep track of how well I'm doing, but this little application
does. There's an app for everything. It's called 'I Am Sober.'"

Jeff spent nearly half his life addicted to drugs and alcohol, "anything that would change how I felt," he says. He now works at The Café, and maybe he's even alive, because he got a second chance. And a third. And a fourth. And, really, too many to count.

The number of Jeff's new chances highlights one of the dilemmas of addiction recovery: How many breaks should Jeff have gotten? And what kind?

Relapses are a fact. One of the formulas for success The Café uses in hiring people with a history of drug or alcohol abuse is to insist that they're in a formal treatment program. Kind of.

"I've been doing this for twenty years, but it's all new to me," says Sal. "It's been a process. I tell myself, and I tell people when I hire them, I don't hire anybody who's in recovery unless they're in some kind of organized program. But I do make exceptions."

Jeff's story describes the paradox of keeping and breaking the rule of insisting on participation in a formal program. Jeff is not his real name. He's enthusiastic about telling the lessons of his story, but that story has touched a lot of people in tough ways, and I'm respecting their privacy.

Jeff says he left a traumatic home life at sixteen and found a job in a chain restaurant as an expediter—the person who takes the plates of main courses from the kitchen and puts the sides and garnishes on them for the servers.

Jeff joined the restaurant party culture that Sal and Cindy found so destructive to their family, even though he always told himself he would never do any kind of drugs.

"Being on my own, surrounded by the wrong people, I went the other way," he says. "I started going to rave clubs and doing Ecstasy. I thought I was having fun just doing it on the weekend. I was really enjoying the people I was around. It made me be able to talk to people better. I could talk to anybody."

Jeff quickly picked up the tricks of the kitchen and became a cook. He learned to tell the difference between a rare and medium-rare steak by touching it. He met a woman who was a bartender and they had a son he hasn't seen since 2011, after "the drug use became something I couldn't control anymore."

Jeff started moving from job to job.

"I didn't really have any goals. It was crazy. I didn't know what I wanted to do in life," he says. "There was so much fog in my head I couldn't even tell you what my interests were. I was seriously on drugs for fourteen years. I know I tried to stop for ten of those years and could never really achieve it."

One of those times he was trying to figure out how to recover, a guy asked if he'd like to make some easy money. "'Just walk into a bank, cash this $5,000 payroll check, and you'll earn 10 percent.'

"It was so easy I just decided to do it again and again. I didn't think about the consequences."

The counterfeiting ring would drop Jeff off near a bank, meet him afterward at a freeway entrance, then disappear into the traffic. His luck ran out when police stopped him, asked for ID, and Jeff took off running.

"I was jumping a lot of fences, back yard to back yard. I could hear the radios behind me. I stepped out of this front yard and it seemed all Louisville was there with guns pointed at me. That's when I realized you can't outrun a radio."

Jeff spent the next three years moving from county jail to county jail, serving out a variety of sentences.

"People would get visits, they would get letters and phone calls, they'd tell people how much they miss them and love them. I didn't have any of that for three years. I felt cold, like I couldn't have feelings anymore for people."

He met a woman in prison and moved in with her when he got out.

"I got right back on drugs. I had a job, but bills started not getting paid. She kept telling me, 'one more time and I'm out of here.' Finally she was done. I really tried to get it together, to get her back, but I couldn't get off the drugs no matter what."

Jeff took a job as a restaurant cook, and after about a year he saw online that a place called The Café was looking for kitchen help. One attraction to moving was that The Café was not open on Sunday. Through Jeff's life one of the habits he tried to maintain was going to church. But for a lot of restaurants needing to make money from brunch service, taking Sunday off was not an option. "I was on drugs, but I quit for a couple weeks, just long enough to make an impression at The Café," says Jeff.

"He was a clean-cut kid, fairly articulate, dressed nicely," says Sal, who was hoping to find someone who could help run the restaurant so he and Cindy, and other employees, could take vacations without shutting down. "He came in full of energy, never stopping, and I was having him do everything. I was training him to do inventory. He had a car so he could run to the store. I was getting people in place to handle things for us when we were gone, and he completed the puzzle."

But the pieces weren't always fitting.

"He would have these pockets where he would let me down," says Sal. "It became clear to me he was using drugs. I'd confront him about it and he wouldn't admit it. He was asking for cash advances and I was trying to help him out."

Jeff says, "I'd get off work, find some drugs, and go home. I isolated myself every day. Stayed in my room. I didn't do anything. Nothing fun. Nothing with anybody. I had one person I always went to for drugs. I never met anybody in parking lots because I didn't want to get caught. I would go up to their house, walk inside, and go straight home. I'd stay there until the morning and do it all over again, every single day. I'd watch TV and just sit there. I had free cable, thank God for that."

❧

The police stopped Jeff one day in December 2017, after watching him walk unsteadily along the streets. "They could tell I was under the influence," he says, so they checked his record. They found a prior arrest, nothing illegal, Jeff says, but by the time he went to jail and got things sorted out, he'd missed work. Looking back on that encounter, Jeff says, "It was like God doing for me what I couldn't do for myself."

Jeff called Sal to report that he'd be back at work in the morning. Sal had had it.

"No you won't," he said, "you're going into treatment."

Sal was torn. Disgusted. Was it even worth taking Jeff to treatment?

"He started out like a champ, then he declined and I fired him. He cleaned himself up and I gave him a second chance. He came back and then he went down the same road again," says Sal. "I had had enough. It was one lie on top of another. I felt that he was a big fat liar and I couldn't trust him."

Cindy watched Jeff's behavior and told Sal that unless he went into a recovery program, he'd be dead.

"Cindy was the one that had to talk me into helping him get treatment," says Sal. "I'd felt used and manipulated. I was just angry."

Still, says Sal, "He was a good employee as long as he wasn't doing the wrong things. My goal was to get him back."

And it was personal.

"I've been a big fat liar in my life," says Sal. "I do believe in second chances. I liked him as a person and he's told me I was the closest thing he's had to a real dad. You can't have someone tell you that and it not make you feel warm and fuzzy."

Sal took Jeff to the detox center at The Healing Place, for five days, Jeff says, of cleaning his body "…from everything. Meth, heroin, cocaine, Xanax, alcohol, weed, you name it. Detox was the flu times a hundred. Part of the reason I stay sober now is because I remember very vividly what it was like. I didn't want to live."

Sal's cell phone rang and rang and rang. Jeff needed this, Jeff needed that. Sal and Cindy knew he had nothing in detox, no shoes, not even a pair of flip-flops. They also knew the only thing he really needed was to get well.

So Sal ignored the calls, forcing Jeff to face his one job of getting clean—except for one evening in late December. "It's Christmas," Sal said to Cindy. "'We've got to do something for this guy.'"

Driving through town, on the way to Christmas dinner at Cindy's sister-in-law's house, they stopped at The Healing Place to drop off a new pair of slippers for Jeff.

⁂

When Jeff got to the point where he could pass a drug test, Sal learned from a member of St. Paul Church about a halfway house with an available bed. Sal paid the initial fee. Jeff stayed there about ten months, occasionally cooking for the residents. "Homemade dishes. I call one of them Dorito casserole. It doesn't sound like it's good, but if you've eaten it, it's actually a real meal. I make it in this really big pan and everybody asks me when I'm going to make it again."

Jeff went back to work at The Café. He especially likes making omelets, "...probably the best in Louisville and Kentucky and Indiana combined," he says, flavoring them with what he calls the secret of a good omelet, "passion."

At The Café, Jeff says he discovered a business where "everybody cared about everybody. And they've been there for so long. I've never seen that before. People have been there ten years, fifteen years, they don't leave. They love it there and I felt that love."

Jeff has his own version of how The Café's business model blends compassion with the bottom line.

"People in recovery can be some of the hardest workers out there because they really have something to prove," he says. "There's so many people who go into jobs for an interview and they have to lie about their past because they don't want that to affect their future. Sal's one of those people you can tell him the truth about everything and he's going to honor you more because you told the truth, and give you a chance when no one else will."

At the halfway house, Jeff said, "This is as happy as I've ever been. I can only imagine what it's going to be like when I leave this house and move into my own place. I'll be able to be what God intended me to be."

Since that interview, Jeff has moved into his own place, with a woman he met through a dating app. She has a daughter he hopes to be able to adopt. "I get to wake up and see a smile," he says. "It's the little things in life that I missed so much of for so many years."

℃

Seventy-five men sat in chairs against the wall, forming a circle facing each other in the basketball-court-sized room on a Wednesday morning, for a regular recovery class at The Healing Place. During this part of the meeting the residents were getting jobs to help run the treatment center, using a hiring technique that a management textbook might call radically innovative, or even outrageous.

For each job, members of the circle would nominate about three candidates. Nominations were not based on skill or ability, but how much the job would benefit the candidate.

Nominating speeches stressed how the job could fill weaknesses in each nominee: "You're kind of restless and you keep to yourself. You'll grow from working in the kitchen with others." Or, "You can't keep your room clean. You'd benefit from being part of housekeeping." Or, "You were making fun of the people who had to clean a clogged toilet. A maintenance job would help you see another point of view."

What if all hiring was done that way?

When nominations closed for each job, each circle member took turns voting. The setting and the process for that recovery class shines light on the hard realities of treatment, as each group member introduces themself with either "I'm an alcoholic," or "I'm an addict." It's an introduction familiar to anyone who's attended an AA meeting.

Among those realities of treatment is that recovery is hard. It's complicated by contributors like genetics, life trauma, and who you hang out with. Recovery takes time—hard data on relapses is hard to come by but generally shows that getting through at least the first year is crucial. One of the reasons recovery takes time is because alcoholism and addiction can physically change the brain in ways that can take years to repair. Then there's the important and practical complication that recovery can be expensive, and medical insurance varies widely in coverage for addiction treatment.

And everybody's different. Casey Wagner's mother had an insight that her family history made her a candidate for alcoholism, so she quit drinking. Jeff's is the more common story you hear in Alcoholics Anonymous meetings, of repeated failures until you can hardly believe the speaker is still alive. Often, they, too, are amazed they're alive, and they will make a point of telling some version of how they know they're one mistake away from losing everything.

Inside The Healing Place building, two separate sections embody the persistence and power of relapsing. The residential section is there because of the time and attention required for successful treatment, including re-entering society with a different set of habits, and even friends. That can take six to nine months. The other section, the first stop at The Healing Place, is the detox center, an open room with rows of beds. In one corner a bulletin board displays photographs of faces of people who came in and left clean, but started using or drinking again, and died.

ᏆᏴ

Doug Scott brings a perspective on addiction and The Café, from having worked for restaurants as well as through his job at The Healing Place, where he's vice president of mission advancement. Like Sal and Cindy, he's seen how the business of serving food can disrupt family life. But he's careful and nuanced about placing blame.

"The restaurant industry is not responsible for addiction. It's an individual's responsibility for addiction," he says. "The restaurant industry doesn't create addiction, it doesn't aggravate it. It's really just a fertile ground because it provides support for it."

"The hours are part if it," Scott says. "Most of that business is four to midnight, so you can party until six in the morning and then sleep all day. There's that culture of conviviality; it's all about fun. There's a bar and there's drinks and there's food."

The culture also provides convenient financing.

"Addiction is expensive, and it's a cash business. So is the restaurant industry," he says. "A server can be flat broke and in withdrawal from their drug addiction at four o'clock in the afternoon but at eleven o'clock that night have enough money to support their habit."

Scott says Sal and Cindy "have developed a business concept that breaks that paradigm of being conducive to addiction." With lack of alcohol and the daytime hours, "It's designed to support more of a traditional employment lifestyle. There's a little more mainstream normalcy."

Saner hours and no bar service might create a safer space for an employee in recovery, but it won't always work, as Sal has found, as Jeff's story shows, and as Scott will tell you from his own story of recovery. He says sobriety can commonly take more than a half a dozen tries. "Hitting bottom" is the commonly used phrase in recovery. Scott describes that as finally getting to the point where the misery of addiction becomes greater than the pain the user is trying to mask with chemicals.

"Everybody has their own path and everybody hits bottom in a different way," says Scott. "For me it was because I was walking the streets of Louisville, homeless and living under a bridge, and my feet were bleeding because I hadn't changed my socks in three weeks."

Scott concedes there's always a risk of relapse in hiring people in recovery, holding himself up as an example. "I'm eleven and a half years sober and all I have is today. I'm one bad decision away."

But he offers a twist on the risk. Scott argues that an employee in treatment offers guarantees that other workers don't.

"A person in recovery has a program that demands that they be accountable, that demands that they be responsible and be truthful," he says. "A person that's in recovery is someone that's highly motivated. They're highly grateful to have another shot not only at being alive, but at a job."

The word "accountability" comes up a lot from people in recovery programs. It's a commitment to not use drugs or alcohol, a commitment to their recovery sponsor for staying in touch, and a commitment to their friends and employers that they will show up on time and follow through on what they said they would do.

Sal sees the value of formal programs that make a priority out of accountability, even though his heart will occasionally overlook some warning signs.

"There's a fine line when you're trying to help people in recovery," says Sal. "You have to have compassion for them but also not enable them to pull the wool over your eyes and run a game on you."

Sal tries to describe one of those fine lines that has to do with the knowledge that recovery takes time: "I don't intentionally hire anybody who is a drug addict or a former drug addict who is not in a program. People come to me and say you're friendly to people in recovery, and if they've been clean for three years and they just want to work in a safe place and they can tell me their story, that's fine. But if somebody says I've been clean for two months and I need a job, I like them to be in some kind of treatment program."

Sal says, "It all goes back to the main thing: we're in the restaurant business and we have to be well staffed. The only thing I can measure is conduct, behavior, and attendance."

Sal's tough talk about what he can measure reveals a central tension between compassion and the bottom line. You can set all the rules you want, but people will be people, coming up with the unexpected. That's why Sal considers working with people in treatment to be a work in progress. A feature of The Café's business model is that it doesn't set out to give second chances. In Jeff's case, Sal wasn't looking to help someone kick a habit; he just needed a cook. Even the soft guideline of wanting recovering employees to be in a formal program didn't work

because Jeff didn't tell Sal about his addictions. When Sal finally reacted to the warning signs that Jeff was breaking the rigid rules, The Café
took a risk on a solution it hadn't tried before. Sal says Jeff is the first
person he successfully got into treatment.

Another advantage of the business model at The Café is that with
several employees in recovery, workers help spot some of those warning
signs.

"My staff knows light-years ahead of me that so-and-so's using and
that we need to do something," says Sal. "They don't want them there.
It brings everybody else down when somebody relapses in their midst."

Sal's learned to watch for red flags like regularly asking to borrow
money or a lot of emergencies in their personal life. Doug Scott recom-
mends reacting quickly to those alarms.

"Don't ignore those early warning signs," says Scott. "Hold employees accountable for their actions if they're not showing up to work
or they're late. Don't sweep it under the rug because you need them to
work the next shift. Meet them head on and address them."

Scott concedes the risks in hiring people in recovery.

"Sometimes you have to go through three, four, five, six, to
get that one, but when you get that one it's like striking gold."
So Scott advises being patient.

If being both patient as well as holding people accountable seem to
contradict each other, Scott has an explanation.

"Show little tolerance to the individual employee, but be patient
with people in recovery as a whole," says Scott. "Don't let the actions
of a few rob you of the opportunity to reap the benefits of an employee
in true recovery."

Scott says The Café's second-chance business model goes beyond
getting good employees. He sees it as a path to easing the addiction
crisis by remaking attitudes toward people in recovery.

"Stigma is real," says Scott. "Our prisons are full of people with drug charges and drug-related charges. They have felonies on their records. Imagine getting out of a treatment facility and getting yourself about a year sober only to be told time and time again, 'I'm sorry, you can't get hired.' What are you going to do? You're going to get high and rob somebody again."

Scott drives home his point about overcoming stigma by telling a story about a TV fundraising appeal for The Healing Place that Scott was holding at The Café. Sal didn't want to call attention to The Café's efforts.

"I had to explain, 'Sal, this isn't about you, it's about getting a message out to the public,'" says Scott. "Having businesses that are willing to hire people in recovery will go a long way to breaking down the barriers of stigma toward addiction. People are dying, slowly, spiritually, physically, in graveyards, dead because as a community, as a nation, as a world, we are afraid to talk about this, to say this is who I am and what I'm doing, to talk about the success, and about the struggle.

"Businesses have a unique responsibility to step up and help remove some of these barriers," says Scott. "Sal will tell you that he's been through dozens of hires, but then he's going to tell you about the ones that have worked out so well. The ones that have not only changed his business but his personal life. That's the story we need to tell."

☙

In April 2018, Jennifer Hancock faced cameras and reporters at the Louisville news conference, standing next to US Senate Majority Leader and Kentucky's senior Senator, Mitch McConnell. Hancock is president and CEO of Volunteers of America Mid-States, a not-for-profit regional housing and addiction recovery organization.

They were announcing federal legislation to fund career training and transitional housing to help recovering addicts find and keep jobs—legislation that would pass Congress and be signed into law later that year.

Hancock introduced two other people—Brandy Lee and Sal Rubino. Lee had graduated from a Volunteers of America treatment program and had just started a job at The Café.

"I've lost everything," Lee told the news conference. "I've lost children, homes, and cars."

She credited The Café with helping put a life back together.

"It's awesome because I've been given a second chance," said Lee. "A lot of employers don't do that."

A few months after that news conference, Lee left The Café for another job—a step made possible, Hancock says, because Sal hired her.

"That launched her into a career path where she gained skills, she gained confidence, she gained income that continued to stabilize her family," says Hancock. "That is a real person whose life is better today because Sal gave her a second chance."

Hancock thinks those chances are too hard to come by for the 20,000 people a year reached by her organization's housing and treatment programs. Like Doug Scott, she sees a stigma that limits opportunity for people in recovery. She says addiction needs to be seen as a medical condition.

"We're all deserving of second chances and we've all had second chances," says Hancock. "For some reason in our society we've separated those who experience the disease of addiction as different from those who experience the disease of cancer or diabetes in terms of whether they're worthy of work. Work is a fundamental aspect of feeling like you're a contributing member of society, so we further marginalize people and therefore promote criminal thinking by segregating people and saying you're not worthy of work based on the kind of disease you have. Addiction is stigmatized as a moral failing, and to me that's just a fundamental flaw in logic that we are still challenged with in our society."

Hancock says that treating addiction recovery like other diseases means acknowledging its causes and cures by taking the time to manage the role of personal relationships and family history, to learn new habits, and even to repair physical damage.

"The first three years of recovery is especially hard because people have to go through a process of relearning a lot of basic skills that most of us take for granted. How to show up to work on time," says Hancock. "Especially for people who have used opioids, there is an impact to their cognitive functions. It takes a good three years before they can use the executive functions of their brains to make sound judgment calls and to use reasoning and logic."

Hancock describes the variety of treatments at Volunteers of America, like residences that allow mothers to keep their children with them, providing group meetings and recovery sponsors, and paying attention to addiction research developments.

"We don't just treat the symptoms," says Hancock. "We treat the root cause, which often is rooted in trauma. The field of addiction treatment has awakened to what is being called a moral injury that has occurred because of the trauma. It calls for a highly therapeutic process that addresses the core issues that have led the person to be vulnerable and become addicted."

For all the good that second chances mean for lives like Brandy Lee's, Hancock says they also help businesses like Sal's.

"It's good for his business because he's finding that people in recovery have a higher level of accountability than the general public because they're following a program that calls for them to be extremely, excruciatingly mindful of how they have harmed people in the past, to repair the wrongs, and to pay forward what has been given to them," she says. "People I know who live a life of recovery are loyal, they are committed, they are resilient, strong, and tenacious. They've overcome something most of us can't imagine having to fight. They can be some of the hardest-working employees there are, and the most creative problem solvers."

Hancock says The Café's business model helps it keep those good workers.

"I see Sal as so much more than an employer," she says. "He has called me because he has had employees who are getting ready to become homeless. Not many employers call me because they're worried about where employees are going to put their heads at night. Sal knows that if someone does not have stable housing, it will threaten their ability to be a good employee. There's a business case for taking care of the whole person and not just their professional side. I know there's also a moral driver and I'm sure a spiritual driver to that for Sal, but he's the kind of employer who doesn't compartmentalize and just care about someone eight hours a day. He takes care of the whole person."

Does God Belong in a Restaurant?

The Café's Country Chicken Salad

Makes 10 servings

[Note: Allow time for chicken to bake and chill before proceeding with recipe and time to chill finished recipe before serving]

Chicken Breast Seasonings:

1/2 tsp salt

1/2 tsp ground black pepper

1/2 tsp ground white pepper

1/2 tsp dried thyme

1/2 tsp dried basil

1/2 tsp dried parsley

1/2 cup vegetable oil

3 lbs. boneless and skinless chicken breast

Salad

1 cup chopped celery, small dice

2 Gala apples, medium size, chopped

1/3 cup chopped pecan pieces

1 1/3 cup mayonnaise

1/4 tsp white pepper

1 tsp granulated sugar

1 tsp salt

2 tsp cider vinegar (if desired; taste before adding)

In a medium-size bowl, mix seasonings with vegetable oil. Coat chicken breast with seasoned oil, mix, and bake in a shallow baking dish at 350°, covered, until done, about 35-45 minutes. Then chill.

Cut chicken breast into 1/2-inch diced pieces.

In a large bowl, mix together chicken breast, celery, apples, and pecans. In a medium-size bowl, mix together mayonnaise and remaining ingredients. Add to chicken mixture.

Chill for two hours before serving.

Most Thursdays at 7:48 a.m. Sal meets with two other men over breakfast at The Café. They chose the time as a light-hearted acknowledgment of one member's penchant for precision. It's called a reunion group and is part of the follow-up program to the Walk for Emmaus Christian retreat, where Sal and Cindy worked out decisions like hiring refugees and closing on Sunday. More informally, it's called an accountability group. But instead of pledging to standards like being clean, sober, and on time for work, like members of substance recovery groups, this breakfast club meets to keep their daily lives accountable to Christianity.

There's not much that is more personal than your own spirituality, and acting on those beliefs, or even talking about them, can get uncomfortable and even dangerous when the internet makes the private public and launches it onto a polarized world stage.

Business owners are particularly susceptible. They navigate additional layers as they pursue a positive bottom line and seek to keep their customers satisfied.

One high-profile path to promoting your business as caring about more than just dollars and cents even has an acronym—CSR, Corporate Social Responsibility. Academic journals and management manuals regularly examine every aspect of CSR, analyzing the profitability benefits to determine whether being responsible brings in money or takes it away from investing in other areas of the company. Popular attention to doing the right thing in business ranges from Google's parent company, which has adopted the well-known motto, "Do the right thing," to a conventional wisdom that younger people are more likely to patronize companies that demonstrate morality, ethics, or social action.

Other businesses take a more direct approach to acting on the religious principles of the owners. They tend to be motivated not so much by whether being responsible can increase income, but by their personal beliefs. The most famous of those get covered in the news for going to court over how they hire and who they choose to serve. Less high-profile practices can run from posting Bible verses on the wall, to declaring their principles in a brochure, to supporting causes or nonprofit groups. Some restaurants have organized to be more socially conscious by acknowledging the rough working conditions in their own industry and to reduce heavy workloads, and to make restaurants friendlier environments for employees in recovery programs.

The goals of The Café didn't start out to be as lofty as any of that. It just needed workers.

"It was total business," says Sal. ""We were just trying to fill positions. That's how we sustain our family. That's where we put the proverbial bread on the table and pay the mortgage, so the business needs to be profitable."

That may explain the we-need-reliable-workers origin of The Café's second-chance hiring practices, but not other decisions, like closing on Sundays and evenings, not serving alcohol, and coming up with management techniques for people who might not meet traditional job qualifications. The Café's full business model developed over the years, with the intertwining of morality, compassion, the desire for family stability, church friendships, and Sal and Cindy's Christianity.

Sal uses the word "organically" a lot to describe that process. When asked whether his Christian faith played a part in his business decisions over the years, Sal leans forward and raises his eyebrows like he's about to reveal a secret to a puzzle he still doesn't understand.

"Only afterwards," he says. "When we look back on how things have evolved, we realized that it was God at work. It wasn't that we were making these decisions informed by faith; it was God at work in our lives that we were totally oblivious to. It was presented to us and we were obedient and we accepted that cross and God has blessed us."

As much as that sounds like an evangelical Christian focused on spreading the message of the Bible, Sal doesn't quite see it that way.

"I struggle with evangelism," he says. "I struggle with things that many Christians are called to because it just doesn't feel natural to me."

Sal talks with confidence about the rules for running a successful restaurant. When it comes to how his faith fits in with the business, he sounds like somebody who's still trying to figure it out.

"Cindy and I didn't come to a full understanding of the Christian faith as we see it today until about the time we started The Café," he says. "So it just doesn't feel genuine or sincere to us to construct The Café and its culture as if we were mature followers of Christ. We're seekers of our faith rather than teachers of our faith."

Sal combines his restaurant knowledge with his faith questions by trying to act as an example rather than proselytizing.

"We're not really a place for Christians; we're a place for everyone," he says. "We try to find God where we are and not to try to construct a temple for him. We're just trying to do our work and doing it in a way that honors him, not through pontificating or Bible thumping, but by being genuine Christians and trying to walk the walk."

Garrison Cox is one of the three members of Sal's Emmaus Walk accountability breakfast group responsible for helping make sure Sal walks the Christian walk. As he sees it, Sal and Cindy practice their faith at The Café not as the showpiece of the business, but as its foundation.

"It's not a Christian bookstore," says Cox. "It's subtle. It's not overt the way their faith is manifested in their business. I think it informs their decisions."

That behind-the-scenes approach makes sense to Tom Grieb, who served as the minister at St. Paul church while The Café was getting started at the Antique Mall.

"Sal and Cindy have an actions-speak-louder-than-words faith, but they're also not at all hesitant to define their actions by a well-placed word about the difference Jesus has made in their lives," says Grieb. Christians commonly debate among themselves how aggressive they should be in recruiting people to their faith. Grieb sees the logic of The Café's approach of acting rather than preaching. "There is a call for us to make disciples, but you and I never win the first person to Christ. God's the one who does the work. Ours is to live a Christlike life."

Grieb talks in the cadences of his role as a minister as he translates what living a Christlike life has meant to the evolution of The Café's business model.

"Ours is a faith of second chances, big-time," he says. "Some employers would say they're not going to deal with some of the people Sal and Cindy hire, but Sal and Cindy saw the potential and what great things they had to offer as employees. The lesson is to make decisions based upon your faith, your core values. The lesson is that you can invest in people that maybe others are not going to invest in. The lesson is don't be afraid to be in a relationship with people."

Cindy says The Café's business model grew out of the restaurant culture they knew of "treating people however you wanted because they were expendable." That use-people-up-and-move-on practice clashed with the discussions they were having with their new friends at church.

"When our faith became so important to us, we knew that we needed to bring that to work every day if we were going to be real about our faith and treat people with dignity and respect and fairness." Those faith principles, she says, had practical benefits. "We got a second chance. Would offering that to someone be something that we would want to develop in our business? Would people respond to that? Could we change the cycle of always having to retrain new people and keep employees longer if a person felt there's something different here? We wanted to see if people would respond if they thought that they didn't have to be treated poorly, no matter if they came from another country as a refugee and didn't speak the language or if they came from a halfway house. They could get a new start."

Cindy sees her Emmaus group as a way to hold her accountable for being "authentically Christian," from living the Golden Rule and treating people the way she would want to be treated, to valuing a person's worth.

"You may be of a different religion, a different culture, and worship in a completely different way than we do, but we're all God's people, and God wants all of us to be on the Earth together," she says. "It's not about judging people on where they are in their world as far as their accomplishments, but appreciating someone just for who they are. Not for what they bring to the table."

The pastor at Crescent Hill Baptist church, where many of Louisville's Karen refugees attend, says restaurants are fitting places for spirituality, and that The Café strikes the right tone.

"When you're in the restaurant business, you're in the spiritual business whether you recognize it or not. You're satiating the stomach's desire but also the desire for connection with other people, and a connection with something that goes unseen," says Jason Crosby. "Sal and Cindy are uniquely and well positioned to do that in a manner that is not ostentatious, that is not down-your-throat Bible-verse beating. It's authentic."

❧

Steve Clark and Annette Ellard hold strong stances on faith in the workplace, even going as far as having a motto for their work. In their position with the Cooperative Baptist Fellowship, they help Karen refugees settle into Louisville society.

"One of the common statements in our culture that I despise is, 'it's not personal, it's just business.' The reality is, everything is personal on some level," says Annette.

Steve adds, "It doesn't give you license to not be living out your Christianity."

Annette argues that any moral code needs to follow the worker into their place of business.

"Regardless of what faith you have or don't have, you can't believe one thing and do another. It will destroy you." says Annette. "For any business and business owner, you have to decide who you're going to be, what you value, and do that. It's common for businesses to have mission statements and values statements. It's not very common for them to truly live those out. I think Sal and Cindy, through The Café, are really trying to live their faith into and through their business.

"Steve and I use as the motto of our ministry John 10:10. 'The thief has come to steal and to kill and destroy. But I, Jesus, have come that they may have life and have it twofold,'" she says. "The Karen and other refugees, they have known the thief. They have literally had a government work to steal and to kill and to destroy them. Sal and Cindy are working against that also, to create the opportunity for a full life for people."

☙

Jennifer Hancock sees similarities between the work of The Café and the work that Volunteers of America does for people who are homeless and in addiction recovery. The first contact was culinary, before The Café and the Volunteers of America offices moved away from the Antique Mall. The neighborhood didn't offer many other lunch options and, says Hancock, "It was just great food. The chicken salad was to die for."

The two businesses grew closer as they learned more about each other and their roles in helping people in substance abuse treatment. Now Volunteers of America regularly calls in catering orders and holds breakfast meetings at The Café. Hancock also sees a similarity in balancing faith and business. Volunteers of America started more than one hundred years ago, growing out of religious traditions. It has a mission of serving all beliefs, if for no other reason than that some of its income comes from government funding.

"We are a not-for-profit business but also a faith-based organization. As such, we have a lot in common with the type of enterprise that sees itself first and foremost as a business with accountabilities to the bottom line, but the way we drive and achieve business success is through processes and strategies that are morally sound," says Hancock. "We avoid evangelizing. We don't proselytize. We welcome people of all faiths and no faith. We want people of all walks of life to feel comfortable here."

Hancock would say that business ethics is not an oxymoron but that it doesn't just happen. Income and morality do fit together, as long as you also do the work of keeping them in balance: overemphasize income and you can end up mistreating people for profit; proselytizing can exclude people with different beliefs.

Yes, that's extra work, and Hancock uses that approach in her organization to do the even bigger work of taking on some of today's most forbidding tasks—homelessness, alcoholism, drug addiction.

When I ask her if all that isn't exhausting and discouraging, she says no and refers to the well-known starfish model. That model is explained as someone seeing thousands of starfish washed up and stranded on a beach, with no hope of saving them all, but knowing that throwing one back into the ocean can at least save that starfish. For Hancock the significance of that story might be explained as the reverse starfish model, where the favor gets returned.

"Changing lives one person at a time is actually the part that keeps me so energized," she says. "It doesn't drain us. We feel inspired." The work of giving people second chances "is not a risk, it is only a benefit."

That's how it worked at The Café.

"We got this business going, we've got this income stream, we thought, why not give these people second chances?" says Sal. "What we found was they changed our lives and perspectives. They were a blessing to us."

CHAPTER 15

The Discipline of Being Nice

You've got to get up every morning
With a smile on your face
And show the world all the love in your heart

—Carole King, "Beautiful"

It's like working on a pirate ship. That's kind of how the crew are in a lot of
restaurants.

—Clark Rubino

James Ryan Coomer got his first job working at The Café. He had an in. The Coomers and the Rubinos knew each other as members of St. Paul church, and Sal and Cindy had watched him grow up. So after Coomer's first year of college his mom suggested he e-mail Sal about a summer job.

"Sal replied really quick," says Coomer. "I don't even remember if he actually interviewed me. It was like, I have to sit here and talk to you for a couple of minutes just to make it look like I'm not just hiring a family friend. He was like, we'll see you at eleven o'clock in the morning."

Coomer started by getting trained as an expediter—"…the last person to see anything that goes out of the kitchen. So they're kind of the quality control check," says Coomer. Over the years he took on other jobs at The Café, liking the flexibility of the schedule that allowed him to attend college. Sal was even tolerant of Coomer as he left to pursue other jobs, rehiring him when they ended or didn't work out.

One day, while Coomer was waiting tables with his normal sense of urgency, on his way to a table he cut in front of a customer on their way to the restroom.

"Cindy pulled me aside and said, 'I watched this happen,'" says Coomer. "She said, 'Don't let it happen again because that's not how we run our business.'"

That story doesn't surprise Sal at all.

"There are rules about walking," he says. "It's in our employee handbook. You always yield to the customer, allow them to walk in front of you. Always offer them to go first, even if you're carrying a tray of food."

There it is, on page 3 of the 17-page Hospitality Standards handbook each employee signs, item #2 under the Maintaining Hospitality heading: "When crossing paths with guest, always yield to the guest, allowing them to pass in front of you."

The lesson of the handbook is that being nice doesn't just happen. For all the compassion Sal and Cindy try to carry out through The Café, their tone turns tough when they talk hospitality. It's a value they each learned from their family as they grew up, and it turned into a discipline through formal schooling and hard-nosed restaurant bosses. That's what James Ryan Coomer ran into that day he cut off the customer.

"Ryan probably looked at me like I had three heads, like, 'What do you mean? I was doing the right thing, I was doing my job,'" says

Cindy. "I pulled him aside and said, 'This is not about you, it's about the guests. They're here to be welcomed and appreciated, not to be bulldozed over by a punk kid.' I don't like that, and the people who taught me that did not like it. They taught a gracious politeness. It's a whole atmosphere taught to me by professionals from the old school serving very high-end people. We were there to fill their water glass when it had the least little bit of water out of it, bring them a fresh napkin. It was bred into us."

If Cindy threw Coomer for a loop at the time, today he says he still carries life lessons from The Café that helped launch him into a colorful career.

The food service industry fascinated Coomer, and he says he might have become a chef if he hadn't been even more interested in theater. From high school and into college he got involved behind the scenes in dramatic production, including lighting and scenic and costume design. After a few years, Coomer disappointed Sal by giving notice. A Broadway production of *Wicked* was coming to town, and Coomer had a chance to help design the harnesses for the flying monkeys.

"Right out of college I got essentially my dream job," says Coomer. "I think Sal was upset that he was going to lose an employee, but he said he was excited to see me succeeding doing what I loved."

Within months Coomer's dream job had become too routine. He went back to The Café, and "Sal took me back with open arms."

Coomer picked up freelance jobs while working at the restaurant.

One of his gigs was at Play Louisville, a nightclub known for its drag shows.

"I had reconnected with a guy I was dating, and we started dating again. He started doing drag, and I build costumes, so I was building his performance outfit and it got him recognition with the local drag queens. They were like, 'Why is this new entertainer so well dressed?'"

Coomer worked late nights and into the mornings, sewing the lavish costumes as well as stage managing at Play Louisville and running the light and sound board. He worked independently for local entertainers, sewed wedding dresses, and, in one notorious case, altered his younger sister's prom dress.

"It was a week before prom and I had taken the dress apart and it was in pieces on the floor," he recalls. "It was just me being in the middle of the process of what I do, but to somebody from the outside it looked like a murder scene, like a dead body on the floor. I texted my sister a picture of it and said, 'Are you ready for prom?' It was entirely under control but I had the chance for a total asshole big brother moment, and I thought, 'I'm going to run with it.' I went and saw her off to prom; the dress fit well. She's smiling in her pictures."

Coomer moved his flair and impishness to California, where he worked on TV shows and a music video and built a costume for a performer on a concert tour with Pink. He also took with him lessons from The Café.

"I learned more than just food," he says. "Skills like how to talk to people. I feel a lot more comfortable approaching people. When I first took over as expediter, I wasn't effectively communicating. It was a hard lesson learned when the tickets pile up and there's a lot of food sitting there, and people are yelling at you. It's a drowning feeling. Sal would ask if I needed him to take over and I would say yes and would see how he talks to the people. You have to have an approachable but very authoritative voice. And you have to find out what's going on and find a compromise."

Part of finding that compromise, Sal says, gets built into the system ahead of time.

"We deliberately engineered our menu so there's always a solution," says Sal. "That's why we created combinations with a cup of soup and a half sandwich and a salad so at least the guest could have something when the kitchen is running slow. You can get them a cup of soup, get them a salad while they're making the rest of the meal."

Coomer learned other lessons during breaks, expanding his world talking with fellow employees. He brushed up on his high school Spanish. Refugees studying for the citizenship test asked for help memorizing the presidents.

"I was like, 'Do you have the cheat sheet because I probably can't name a dozen presidents.' It takes a lot for them to become a full citizen. I got an appreciation for people who naturalize into the United States."

Employees in recovery opened his eyes to another set of struggles new to him.

"I was having lunch with this woman who was flippantly talking about her time in prison and I was like, 'You must have been there for a couple of nights,' and she's like, 'oh no, no, no. Jail is where you spend a couple of nights. Prison is where you're locked up for a while,'" says Coomer. "It definitely taught me to enjoy things sparingly when I go out and party or drink with friends because I don't want to go down the path some of them did. I built relationships with them. They are great people; it's just that life hit them at the wrong point in the wrong way. They're still good people. It was a life-changing experience."

At The Café, Coomer found an employer supportive in another way.

"I said, 'Hey Sal, my boyfriend needs a job, do you think you could hire him?' Sal had this attitude that he would find some way to put him to work, so Kevin and I got to work together at The Café. That was pretty cool," Coomer says. "While we were working there, there was another gay couple working there. Sal and Cindy are non-judgmental towards anybody's religion or anybody's nationality or life story of how they ended up in recovery; that was the least of their concerns. They brought Kevin and me in just as they would anybody else."

Ryan didn't get treated like anyone else, though. Cindy says she grades on a curve.

"I think he saw that everybody is worthy here, but I held him to a different standard because I knew his family and he came into this job knowing what we're about," she says. "I'd tell him not to sit around and talk to your buddies. Do your job. Do what we trained you to do. I think he knew I still cared for him and I wanted the best for him. I hate to see people make mistakes and fail. I wanted him to stay true to the person he was trying to grow into."

Coomer learned the standards of The Café and saw how it met those standards. He adopted them.

"I've seen Cindy nitpick and do quality control, like, 'these grapes aren't fresh enough. The tomatoes have been sitting in the juice at the bottom so they're mushy and not what we expect,'" he says. "You get frustrated, but it instilled in me a sense of quality control, so even when she wasn't there I would say, 'No, this isn't what Cindy wants. We need to go back and fix this.' They're there to support you and have fun with you, but they'll keep you in check and let you know if you're not doing things and maintaining the standards. They expect those standards because that's what's gotten them to where they are."

Creating that sense of ownership is exactly what Cindy was after. If The Café had a staff organization chart, it wouldn't include boxes for management jobs. Instead, employees worked their areas until they absorbed the quality and teamwork standards Sal and Cindy expected. That doesn't happen by accident.

"I'm friendly to people, but when you're on my clock, you work on my clock. I'm going to hold you accountable for how much time you spend on a smoke break," says Cindy. "I expect you to be in charge of your area. But also to be part of the team you have to go do something unselfishly for the team. It might be taking a bin of dirty dishes to be emptied rather than waiting for somebody else. You motivate people by ownership of their job and by them owning the part that they play."

One management tip Coomer learned from Cindy came down to a single phrase—*mise en place*, a common cooking term from French for having everything in its most useful location. It means having all your ingredients chopped and in position, "to keep things efficient in the kitchen," says Coomer. "The benedictine is on the line next to the tomato and cheese because the same person that makes the benedictine sandwiches is also making the pimento cheese sandwich."

Coomer still thinks of that phrase because of its similarity to a phrase he knows from theater, *mise en scène*, French for putting on stage. It refers to the location of the actors and props in a theater production. For Coomer, both terms mean "being able to manipulate the elements I have at my disposal and making sure that all of those are properly in place to assist with the efficiency and a stronger final product. I learned from Cindy and, still today, I gather my anticipated supplies needed for a project before I begin instead of waiting until I need them, which helps me with my sewing."

Restaurant work regularly raises theater references. Sal and Cindy refer to the business as an orchestra, coordinating conductor and players. In The Café's living room-sized kitchen, which seems even smaller because it's crammed with coolers and ovens and warmers and counters, the cooks move ballet-like as they hoist bread trays and turn with frying pans without colliding with the half-dozen others moving just a few feet away.

Hospitality, says Cindy, is another part of the show.

"It's like acting," she says. "You have to step out of yourself and take on a persona, especially if you're more of a shy, quieter personality. It's a servant mentality. It's not just about you."

❦

Sal gathered the restaurant staff in the quietest corner of The Café, farthest from the customers, which wasn't too hard at 10:30 a.m., the slowest time, between the breakfast and the lunch crowds. Coomer had long since left for his job in California, but he would have recognized the gathering as "one of those times when Cindy or Sal would say, 'We've seen a crack in the foundation of what we stand on, and we've got to fix it.'"

The servers had been complaining that the greeter played favorites in assigning servers the best tables. Sal was trying to move away from being the only greeter, and he thought he'd found a good person to fill the spot. But to make that possible, he needed everyone to get along.

Sal opened the meeting by holding a small Bluetooth speaker and playing the opening to the Carole King song, "Beautiful":

You've got to get up every morning
With a smile on your face
And show the world all the love in your heart
Then people gonna treat you better
You're gonna find, yes you will
That you're beautiful, as you feel

A couple of the employees knew the 48-year-old song, recorded before they were alive. Others had heard it on TV and asked who the artist was. Sal pivoted to the employee handbook, referring to a line drawing on the cover. It shows two images, a smiley face and a dollar sign, with arrows connecting them.

"The dollar sign represents income because everybody works for income. The smiley face represents enjoying your job and looking forward to coming to work. If you don't enjoy your job, you're not going to be a happy person, and no good can come from that."

Ahead of the meeting Sal had created a spreadsheet that showed customers were in fact being distributed fairly among servers, contradicting the complaints. The hostess said she wasn't out to get anybody and wanted the team to work together. Sal told the group that his directions to the hostess "are that you don't make decisions how to seat guests according to the needs of our employees. You make decisions based on the needs of the guests. If you go into a restaurant, you shouldn't see the receptionist trying to do some calculation of 'where am I going to put these people' depending on which server's turn is next. That shouldn't happen at The Café."

⁊

In the experience of Sal and Cindy's oldest son, Clark, restaurants tend to attract transient workers with a variety of life goals. The hours are unusual. The skills you learn allow you to pick up and get a job at another restaurant across town, or across the country. While the late celebrity chef Anthony Bourdain called restaurants "the last refuge of the misfit," Clark puts it differently: "It's like working on a pirate ship. That's kind of how the crew are in a lot of restaurants."

Statistics show that as well. While business employee turnover rates tend to be around 40 percent a year, restaurant industry studies come in around 60 or even 70 percent. The Café's turnover matches the industry, but with a difference that tells two stories. One of those stories is the number of long-term employees in key positions—11 years, 13 years, 14 years, 17 years. That longevity comes from a business model built around recognizing the workers' lives beyond the restaurant. That approach doesn't always keep good people around—support for Ryan Coomer's career meant watching an employee come and go.

The other story told by The Café's employee turnover rate is that enforcing quality standards can require a higher turnover rate. As one of the members of Sal's Emmaus Walk accountability group puts it, "Sal is not a pushover. He fires more people in a year than you or I would fire in a lifetime. But not randomly and not unless there's a warning. He's a hard-nosed pragmatist at getting a day's work out of every person."

❧

Sal felt the Carole King meeting went well. He posted the song's lyrics at the workstations. He dwelled on the smiley face/dollar sign graphic as a yin and yang that affect each other. The power of the interplay between those two forces, he says, determines nothing less than both a worker's quality of life and the profitability of their employer.

"You have to enjoy your job and you have to feel like your income is at least adequate. At this level of restaurant worker, it's not about getting wealth, but you have to be making ends meet and not living paycheck to paycheck. If you enjoy your job and you're making money, everything is peachy. If those two things are not in balance, then things are going to unravel for you, and that affects the business."

Tips bring a different dynamic to a workplace, where "a smile on your face" shows up faster and more directly than in other businesses.

"A server going around a sourpuss all day will contribute to co-workers' relationships. It's going to contribute to how much they get in tips," he says.

In staff meetings and individual meetings, Sal preaches about the uniqueness of restaurant work, and of The Café.

"In this business you have to take the good with the bad. Some days you work three hours and you walk out with $80 cash in your pocket. Where are you going to go get a job like that?"

Sal wants them to connect their job with his larger vision.

"At The Café, our business philosophy revolves around our guests—to give them the best food, the best service, and the best value so that they want to return. It's not about you. This café does not revolve around you. Not that you're not important, because having a good team that works together is part of the secret."

Or as it says in the employee handbook, right above the smiley face and the dollar sign, "We expect you to participate in a system to maintain hospitality with our guests and your coworkers."

While Sal says restaurants are a different breed of business, one way they're the same as other businesses is they're made up of two sides—production, as in the kitchen, and sales, as in the servers. "When people work together, there's always conflict," says Sal.

Facing conflict can be awkward in a restaurant. Finding time and space away from customers can be impossible without asking employees to come in early, or cut into other personal time by staying late. So meetings to restore the balance between money and happiness happen more commonly one-on-one, and in private.

"I tell the employees, 'If you're ever not enjoying you job, I'd like you to tell me.'"

It might sound delusional to think an employee will tell their boss they don't like their job, but Sal insists it can and does work.

"They don't come out and express it exactly that way," says Sal. "But I let them know my door's open and I can always help them. It happens all the time. They bring something to my attention, we can fix it, and they can start enjoying their job."

Sal says he's also learned that, for employees to come talk to him, he has to be ready to hear what they have to say.

"If I'm going help them gain new insights and perspectives on a problem, I've learned over the years you can't do that without listening to them, because a lot of times your prepared solution is flawed. It might not contain important knowledge that you need to hear. If you listen to them first and allow them to share what's on their heart, then you can modify your prepared advice." He offers an example. "Early in my career I brought an employee into my office for being late and missing work. I started laying into her about responsibility and communication, blah, blah, blah, and she sat there with tears in her eyes and told me how her dad had passed away. He was young, it was unexpected. What a heel I was. I was caught off guard and realized from that point forward I had to give people a chance to talk first."

Sal might have realized he needed to listen more and talk less, but as with other "aha!" moments in his life, getting good at it would take practice. He got more lessons as he worked with Cindy to repair their marriage and family and to restart his career. "I've tried to reinvent myself into being less of a talker in everything I do: raising children, being a grandfather, a father-in-law, and all aspects of my personal life."

℘

Sometimes a clash between employees gets resolved by Sal helping each of the workers understand the others' point of view. "I've always been a peacemaker," he says, recalling the speech he made to his high school student body that got him elected class president. Sometimes money is the problem. "I tell them that if you're a good server and you're efficient and you're friendly and you have good hospitality skills, you're going to make money at The Café. It's important to us that you make money and that you're happy. It will happen. We're a busy restaurant. There are plenty of guests to go around. Once you have gained some level of seniority, you can start picking up more shifts, you can work longer shifts. There are lots of ways to increase your income, but it's not going to come by whining and complaining. It comes by service to others, to the team, to the guests."

The Carole King meeting lasted less than fifteen minutes and didn't end with any sort of group rallying cry. Several of the employees commented; the hostess spoke. They talked about service to the customers and returned to work. "The meeting went astonishingly well," said Sal. Eventually, one of the servers who had complained found another job and left The Café.

"Sometimes it's just not fixable," says Sal. "Maybe you need to go someplace where you're going to be happy. We did express that at the meeting. I don't want them to think all they've got to do is come and tell me and I'm going to wave a magic wand and it's all going to go away. Everybody has to participate and work. I can be the catalyst or the coach that helps you see what you can do to make things better, but it's not about me fixing it. It's about us working together to resolve these issues."

Sal's seen the dysfunction of unresolved issues.

"I remember working in places where I didn't want to go out in the dining room because I'd be facing customers wanting to know where their food is, and I didn't want to go back in the kitchen because I'd be facing an angry chef who would tell you to get out of here, I'll tell you when it's ready. So you end up hiding in the bathroom just to avoid the stress of nowhere to go," he says. "I don't ever want to have that. Having things running like clockwork is everything. Our responsibility as owners and management is to create a work environment that people look forward to coming to every day."

Carole King's lyrics live in Sal's head during hiring and firing.

"It's not the people you fire that cause problems, it's the people you don't fire," he says. "Sometimes you hire the wrong people, they don't know how to be happy and find the joy within, and that has to be addressed. They either get with the program or get gone. Having the right systems in place so that things go smoothly is a big component to having a work environment that you can look forward to. The employee has to bring something to the table, too. They have to have joy in their heart."

"You find that out in the interview process," says Sal. "I talk to them about what their hobbies are, what they do when they're not at work. I try to get to know them. They've got to be able to make eye contact, have a nice smile, be able to talk about themselves. We hire a number of people in recovery programs, but that doesn't mean they don't have a life. They're mothers, they're dads, they're brothers, they're sisters. They have the ability to smile even though they've had a tough time and they've made bad decisions. They're still human."

"My favorite interview question is 'What is the most important thing to you in a job?' What I'm looking for is the truth. The truth is usually 'money,' or 'I enjoy my job.' If they say something like, 'That I'm able to take care of my customers,' they're just saying something they think you want to hear. Then I have to probe further and get them to be real. I want them to tell me, 'Getting along with my co-workers.' That's real. Or 'A boss that appreciates my contribution. Being understood.' That's real."

☙

Myra White is one of those long-term employees who carry out the culture of The Café. She started in 2006, after retiring from a twenty-nine-year career as a schoolteacher. She anchors the carry-out section of the restaurant, readies the sometimes hundreds of box-lunch orders for the next day, tallies receipts at the close of business, makes iced tea, bakes cookies…fills in what's needed. She sees how a workplace that people look forward to coming to each day can come down to a matter of a kind word. Or avoiding an unkind word.

"Cussing doesn't happen here," says White. "In the kitchen Cindy doesn't tolerate that. She would let you know if something wasn't appropriate. She would tell you, and if it didn't change you might be fired. They say this is the way they want things to be, and you either do it or, if you don't want to do it, you move on."

Sal says civility among employees is a purposeful part of the kind of business they want to run.

"We discourage the use of foul language," he says. "Cindy and I have worked in restaurants with a culture of thinking the way you get things done is by being mean and pushy. But it's not necessary. You can actually run a kitchen without dropping the f-bomb every other word." He pauses, seeming to realize that that kind of preaching can be tough to practice, and admits, "If anyone does swear around here, it's usually me."

Long-time employees like White also help keep things under control by being able to pitch in outside their main work responsibilities. That, too, says Sal, is deliberate.

"Things get done in a melodic, symphonic way of cooperation, and in order to have that intuitive exchange between co-workers, everybody has to be trained. And not just in one job, but cross-trained in as many jobs as possible," he says. He describes employees "who can flow through the kitchen and work different stations. They might know we're about to run out of chicken salad, so they make the chicken salad and put it in the refrigerator. They look up and see twenty tickets hanging on the salad line, so they jump on the salad line. They might carry the food out to a server or go out front and greet the guests. That's where that intuitiveness comes in, just by being aware, having been trained."

One line in The Café's training manual probably needs more emphasis, the way Sal talks about it. Maybe it should be underlined, or in boldface. It lurks under the heading of "SERVING," item #11: "If your guests experience an unreasonable delay, notify management, so that a manager could go to the table to apologize and serve as a facilitator to get the food out ASAP."

Actually, Sal doesn't even want the problems to get that far.

"One of the things I tell all my new hires—and I restate it with my staff—one of the things I don't want anybody to do, to the point of you're going to lose your job because you've been warned, is not asking for help when you need it," he says. "If you as a server are really busy and a customer gets up from the table and comes over and grabs me and says, 'We've been here for an hour and we haven't got our food—can we have it to go?' then I'm being told I'm losing a customer because you didn't ask for help. You were in the weeds, you knew it, and you didn't come soon enough to prevent this from happening. This is told to them and drilled into them. People have a natural tendency to say they don't need help, I can do this, so we have to train that out of them. We let them know our customer's service is more important than their pride."

❧

Sal will tell you that the different reasons people give for coming to The Café are a deliberate result of the restaurant's broad commitment to quality. The food is the main thing; some more specifically cite the cakes, others that it gives second chances to refugees and addicts. Yet another common refrain goes, "Ooh, it's Sal and Cindy. Especially Sal, for chatting at every table."

Sal says it's all that.

"We offer the total package," he says. He describes chicken from whole fresh chicken breasts, turkey breast roasted in-house. "I try to get around to all the tables and get to know people, and some people think that's important." Employees are told to sit in a quiet corner to eat during their lunch break. "Eat like a human. Standing up behind the station and eating gets seen by guests, and it just doesn't look right. I don't want them to draw attention to themselves." Even the background music from the 1940s contributes, he says. "It's not relevant to one demographic group; it's obscure enough that it's truly background music. It kind of goes with our cuisine that's supposedly comfort food. We have a vintage vibe with the antiques, so we have vintage music. It also kind of goes along with the posters on the walls of Broadway musicals."

One long paragraph in the handbook discourages cell phone use during working hours. Another instructs servers to "Greet guests you will be serving with eye contact, a sincere smile, and a personal greeting within one minute of them being seated." And, "Make a number of contacts and maintain a dialogue with your guests throughout the meal period to insure you are attentive to your guest's needs."

On Sal and Cindy's time off, they have trouble going out to eat. They can't avoid overanalyzing the food and service. They get especially put off by indifference.

"We train our staff to be friendly and hospitable, making our guests feel welcome and appreciated. That is part of our core belief," says Sal. "These days you go into some restaurants and there's this sort of coolness that seems more important than hospitality. We're the antithesis of that. We celebrate friendliness and hospitality. What's wrong with being nice?"

Sal and Cindy spent a lifetime trying to answer that question. They turned it into a set of rules in employee manuals, and a business model. Being nice only begins with a smile. Keeping customers, and employees, means turning nice into a discipline. They learned it means enforcing the employee manual; that making a customer smile over a piece of cake means working with a kitchen employee to make sure the recipe gets followed exactly, day after day after day. It means figuring out when to give an employee another chance and when to fire them. It means telling an employee that it's not about them.

Arriving at that bigger and deeper definition of being nice took work and risk: being patient with refugees learning English or subbing for them when they took extra time off to visit relatives overseas; hiring an alcoholic; driving an employee to a detox center; attending a high-school orientation with a refugee mom and her child.

Sal and Cindy learned they needed to take those lessons home with them and put them into practice with their family. They learned they needed to pay attention to the person behind the title of spouse or child. They learned to rely on church friends who would monitor how their faith was matching up with their personal and work worlds. They learned you could run a business with a heart.

CHAPTER 16

Endings and Beginnings

On July 23, 2019, Sal and Cindy signed papers selling The Café.

As with many big decisions, no single explanation covers all the reasons for taking such a huge step.

One version of the reasoning starts years earlier, when developers eyed the raggedy neighborhood as a new cultural center. The organization that runs downtown's Kentucky Center for the Performing Arts building, home to Louisville Orchestra concerts and traveling Broadway theater, wanted a space to book smaller acts. Plans for the area in addition to the new performance building included space for outdoor gatherings, a brew pub, and repaving one of the streets in quaint-looking brick. The Café would move across the street into an expanded Louisville Stoneware pottery building.

Another explanation starts from decades earlier, when Cindy's dad, George Clark, figured out that his Burger Queen restaurant business needed to be about real estate as much as food. Sal and Cindy relearned that lesson at The Louisville Antique Mall when they realized that, as leaseholders, they couldn't count on The Café for either stable employment or financial security. After the years of financial struggle that drained their bank accounts, they needed a better retirement plan than owning a collection of used restaurant equipment.

And Sal and Cindy were tired. As worthy as their business model was, it took a toll. Years of investing time and emotion into employees and their families who were adjusting from an addiction, an embattled country, or just life, proved as exhausting as it was exhilarating.

"There are all these families that you're responsible for that work for you," says Sal. "Some people can work at that pace until their late eighties. Everybody's wired a little bit differently."

The restaurant business also takes a physical toll. Early morning hours, lifting food containers, circulating through the dining room to chat with diners. "My body aches, standing on concrete for so long." Cindy says. "Sal can't do it much more."

A few weeks after the sale, a crew from a local TV station set up for a remote broadcast from The Café to promote "Dining Out for Life," an event that designates a day for a group of restaurants to donate part of their earnings to benefit HIV/AIDS treatment programs. For the first time in all the years The Café has hosted the broadcast, Sal and Cindy weren't there.

Instead they sat in a coffee shop a mile away, drinking frothy lattes from oversized mugs and talking about their new life.

"Sal would have normally been there at four a.m.," says Cindy. "I would have come in and made the food so the TV reporter could present it and talk about it."

In place of Sal and Cindy, two new managers chatted to the camera—Christy Strauss, the general manager, and kitchen manager Shawn McGuinness.

"We've done Dining Out for Life for twenty-something years," says Cindy. "Somebody else needs to be doing that, not us. Christy and Shawn are gung-ho about having an opportunity to speak."

As Christy and Shawn bantered with the TV reporter about whether the topping for the French toast should be pronounced "syrup" or "serp," Cindy reflected on how the transition would pass along not just a business ownership, but new careers and a new enthusiasm to a new generation.

"They're proud of what they do and they have the energy level. It's exciting to see them happy to get up at four a.m., go in after long hours the day before, and show off what they do. I had that excitement at one time."

Sal sees the changes as an essential next step for The Café.

"To have a successful business, even if you keep the concept pretty much the same, you still need to keep things fresh and alive. Bringing young blood in to do that is really key."

And Sal and Cindy have two young grandchildren they'd like to spend more time doting on than full-time restaurant ownership allows. Sal says, "You're never promised tomorrow."

❧

In the months after the sale, construction crews started transforming the neighborhood around The Café into Louisville's new hot spot. The area right outside The Café would become a small urban park, even hosting an ice-skating rink in the winter. Next to that green space a 2000-capacity performance center would open—Old Forester's Paristown Hall, named for one of the long-time whiskey brands that's part of the revived attention to the region's Bourbon heritage. Its opening concert would feature the high-energy New Orleans musician Trombone Shorty.

The Café's new location across the street would be connected to the Louisville Stoneware building. The upper floors of the complex would be office buildings. The dilapidated shop Sal and Cindy turned into a restaurant twelve years earlier would become a food hall. Local chefs would set up spaces in the building that would open onto the green space in front of the Paristown Hall building.

Whether this explosion of trendiness was the intentional conclusion of Sal's vision for the area, or just luck, the ability to sell a now much more valuable piece of property allowed Sal and Cindy a path to the next part of their lives.

"We had been looking for an exit strategy," says Sal. "Twenty years ago, in the prime of our life, we were faced with possibly losing everything. We don't have a stock portfolio. All of our investment is in this business."

But that kind of investment is one that isn't guaranteed to pay off. One way that family businesses move forward is for the kids to take over, but Sal and Cindy's three children had launched lives that did not involve restaurants.

"That's what happens in a family business," says Sal. "When the children aren't interested you have to figure out other options. Succession planning takes a lot of energy and money, so it made more sense for us to sell."

And that's where Sal recalls Cindy's father advising him that "McDonald's is not in the restaurant business. McDonald's is in the real estate business. They use the restaurant business to grow the real estate business."

Sal had turned that tip into an action plan after his unsuccessful attempts to renew The Café's lease at the Antique Mall.

"It was an awakening for me," says Sal. "Without owning real estate, we really didn't have anything to sell. Purchasing the Paristown building was an insurance policy for us that at some point we'd be able to sell it. It was definitely a retirement plan."

Cindy's father had offered another essential nugget of nuance to restaurants and real estate.

"He told me the tenant creates the value in the restaurant," says Sal. "Property without a tenant is virtually worthless. If you have a good restaurant operator, that piece of real estate's going to be worth more because the tenant is driving the sales so they can afford to pay the rent. As a tenant, you create the value of that real estate, so it behooves you to own that real estate."

While that all sounds like a steely-eyed business plan, The Café's management style presented potential buyers with a tough act to follow. Giving employees second chances at life, shepherding them through addiction treatment, helping them learn English, giving them rides home from work, visiting their homes for traditional meals from other countries, might not be the best business model to attract investors.

It's a complication Cindy says was worth it. "When I see the people who came to work for us and where we were and where they were, we built this thing and we both benefited in so many ways. We gave them the freedom to be their own bosses. They in turn are very loyal and responsible to us. The time has come to say, 'We did it.'"

☙

One of The Café's kitchen workers went on to run her own restaurant—until she learned some of the same hard lessons that Sal and Cindy learned.

Dikura Bhanderi—everybody calls her Deepa—spent the first six years of her life with her parents on a farm in Bhutan, a country less than half the size of the state of South Carolina, with about the same population as Memphis, Tennessee, located between China and India. Her family spent the next seventeen years in a refugee camp in the nearby country of Nepal.

In the early 1990s the Buddhist government, wanting to protect the country's culture, enacted citizenship rules that led to violent clashes and the creation of more than 100,000 refugees in what the Amnesty International human rights group called "one of the most protracted and neglected refugee crises in the world."

Deepa and her family were among the more than 80,000 approved for resettlement to the United States.

"I was so excited and so happy," she says. "We heard we could get a job there. In a refugee camp it's very limited."

A year earlier, Deepa's younger brother had been selected for resettlement and at random was sent to Louisville. So that's where the rest of the family chose when asked. Now parents, an aunt, an uncle, and another brother "live in one big neighborhood."

Deepa interviewed with Sal and started as a dishwasher. A week later she moved to a food prep position and worked in the kitchen for the next four years. The work came easy, she says. She could follow a recipe and had done plenty of cooking in the refugee camp. "We didn't have restaurants," she says.

Deepa never took a class to learn English. She says she picked it up by talking with people, especially at The Café. That's easy to believe after only a few minutes of talking with her. She has a cheery, melodic voice and enough charm to overcome any language barrier. She credits The Café for being a workplace with a camaraderie conducive to learning a new language.

"Everybody loved it there," she says. "We'd get together, we'd talk together, we'd work together. Everybody's cooperative. Cindy and Sal were always with us, we were always happy. It's really nice work."

Deepa recalls getting to know Cindy. They would talk about their backgrounds as they worked together closing up The Café each day.

"Cindy and I worked at the same table and we'd talk like this about our families," she says, with a quick, high laugh that, more than words, can explain how close they became. "Cindy was baking, I would make food for catering, and Sal would deliver it."

What Cindy remembers from those evenings was Deepa's energy, leaving the restaurant to go home and take care of settling a half dozen relatives from the refugee camp into a new country where they didn't know the language or the customs.

"She was in charge of getting everybody situated in the medical system, all their paperwork," says Cindy, bobbing her head in amazement. "I would take her home in the afternoon because we were the last two to clean up together. She worked a full-time job in the kitchen and then she would go home and have another full-time job waiting on her at home. She was only twenty. It floored me, all she was juggling, and when she came to work she acted like it was nothing, compared to a refugee camp."

One January day a blizzard covered Louisville with cold and snow, and Sal and Cindy's son Clark showed up at Deepa's house with a blanket, space heater, food, and fruit. Why are you doing this? she asked him. We have jobs; we're making money. Clark told her that she was part of the family.

Meanwhile, while Deepa worked for The Café by day and helped her family at night, 1,800 miles away in Hollywood, California, Tek Nath Nirouna was looking for a wife with restaurant experience. He'd spent six years as a Buddhist monk in Bhutan, and during the violent political disputes there, he was allowed to relocate to the United States in 2007. He says he quickly learned the restaurant business and ran Indian and Thai restaurants.

Deepa and Tek came from a culture of arranged marriages. "I didn't know him before we were married," she says. Tek's contacts carried news of his search for a wife from his home in California to Deepa in Louisville, and she gave notice in late 2014 that she was leaving The Café.

"The last day everybody looked very sad. I don't like to say good-bye," says Deepa. "At The Café there were refugees from Burma and Cuba. I was the only one from Bhutan. Everybody loved me."

Tek came to Louisville for the wedding, then took his bride back to California. She didn't like the place. The cost of living was too high. Too many people. Deepa was pregnant, and by the time their son was born in 2016 the couple was living in Louisville. A year later they opened the Himalayan, an Indian restaurant along the busy Bardstown Road just two miles from The Café. Business was good, but the long, family-unfriendly hours and trouble finding employees who could help out in the kitchen took their toll. After two years, they sold the restaurant.

"We are very happy not to have a restaurant any more," says Deepa. "We worked very hard. I'm so tired now."

Tek got a job at an Amazon shipping center. Deepa plans to take care of her parents and four-year-old son. After saving for years, they bought a house. Maybe after a year or so or resting they might start another business, maybe a grocery, but not a restaurant, she says. "The restaurant business is too much work."

On a crisp fall day two months before Deepa and Tek sold the restaurant, Sal met me at the Himalayan to introduce me to the owners. Sal was in a relaxed mood, having finalized the deal to sell The Café just a couple months before. While we waited for Deepa, we split an Indian beer—it comes in quart-size bottles—and chatted with Tek. He talked with a droll cadence and half smile about why he became a monk and lived in a monastery. "I was not a good guy," he said with a slight, sly smile alluding to a less-than wholesome lifestyle he left behind for the monastery. "But I was not that much of a bad guy."

Deepa showed up, dark-haired, with a broad smile projecting a personality that seemed to arrive at the table six feet before she did. She told Sal the restaurant was doing well. The hardest part, she said, was finding employees. When Sal told her he had to leave for another appointment, she was disappointed.

"You don't want to eat anything? You have to hurry to go?" she said.

"We'll come back," said Sal. "I'll send you a text or call you. Is your phone number the same? Do you have the same name, did you take your husband's name?"

"Same phone number," she answered as though there was no question they would be friends forever. "Same name. Same Deepa."

℘

The Café's new owners knew they were buying a highly personal business model that had been designed over the years to match Sal and Cindy's goal of making a priority of their family. They bought it with the aim of preserving its culture and character. But there would also be changes. When The Café reopened across the street it would be for seven days a week as well as evenings, and it would serve alcohol.

Would that affect the essence of The Café? Or would that just expand it to a wider audience, bringing back the Sunday brunch crowd, attracting concertgoers for dinner and a drink before or after a concert just a few steps away in the new performance building?

It's a question Sal sees as one that combines the Rubino's business life with their personal lives.

"Every decision you make has a cost. What is the cost of adding dinner? What is the cost of adding Sunday service? What is the cost of adding alcohol?" he asks. "For us the costs were too great, so we were consciously making decisions that were about quality of life and not the income potential. We gave up our quest for fortune and glory, reinvented ourselves, and said, 'Let's try to be happy.'"

While that sounds clear and confident, Sal and Cindy turn more thoughtful as they reflect on a question they were asked by one of their employees in recovery: When The Café started opening evenings and serving alcohol, would it still be a safe place for people in treatment?

The answer at first seems harsh and flip but is actually nuanced, subtle, and goes to the heart of why The Café's management practices succeeded as a business model: Sal and Cindy didn't close evenings and stop serving alcohol in order to help workers in recovery; they did it for themselves. Giving people second chances and treating them like the complex people they are wasn't the point; it was the means to success by all measures of success—business, personal, and spiritual. Sal and Cindy sought to bend the conventional wisdom of the restaurant industry into a lifestyle that supported rather than undermined their family, their faith, and their sense of right and wrong.

If that sounds like it's leaving employees in recovery without support, Sal and Cindy would disagree. They feel they've offered an example that shows a person can succeed while sticking to their values.

Cindy explains that even with the daytime hours and lack of alcohol at The Café, "People still went out after work. Those who wanted to have a drink would get together at a bar afterwards."

What The Café offers, she says, is that "we showed employees you can be part of a restaurant and be part of a group and you don't have to go party your brains out all night. Cindy and Sal don't go out and do this. It's cool to be who you are."

Sal explains that the safe space The Café offers isn't a place without alcohol, but an attitude.

"We try to nip negativity in the bud when it occurs," says Sal. "We try to promote positivity."

୧୬

The Café's legacy in the community is not news to the new owners. Wes Johnson, Jr., and Mike Kapfhammer grew up in Louisville, working in family restaurants. They own four restaurants, including Buckhead Mountain Grill, a local chain with three locations, serving craft beers and a range of dishes from burgers and chicken potpie to salmon and meat loaf.

Johnson analyzes The Café's business model as "one that is guaranteed not to be able to continue in its current form because it is wholly tied to Sal and Cindy as individuals. They purposely created a schedule—to be closed on Sundays, to not open for dinner—that allowed them to live the life they wanted to live at home and be present in the restaurant literally all the time it was open. They worked their butts off to be here all the time."

Johnson calls that "a simple idea that's very difficult to execute, but it's also super powerful. It's their unwavering dedication to making the business work and doing whatever it took to make it work themselves."

Making their business work for their family includes leaving the business, he says.

"So often it happens in small businesses there's no exit strategy," he says. "So many independent restaurateurs and businesspeople die in their work shoes. They don't get the opportunity to pass it on, to realize the value that they've created. I admire Sal and Cindy for being able to realize the financial benefits of what they've created over the years. It's really the story of the American Dream."

Johnson credits Sal and Cindy with helping spark the Paristown development that made the sale possible. Another essential ingredient to the sale, he says, are the expanded hours and bar service.

"The real opportunity to grow Paristown as a neighborhood and as a destination started with the vision that Sal and Cindy had twelve years ago locating the restaurant here," says Johnson. "In order for them to sell this business and move on, it would have to be put in a position where it can grow from a long-forgotten corridor to a growing and bustling development."

But Johnson and Kapfhammer didn't buy just any business that they wanted to expand; they bought The Café. Johnson says, "Sal and Cindy have created not just a restaurant that has great food, served quickly with a smile, that's the same every time; they've created a culture. We want to respect and maintain the process they've created. It's really a lot of what we bought from them. We'd be crazy to come in and say, 'Oh, we know better.'"

The puzzle, says Johnson, is "How do we keep The Café the same and grow it under new ownership and leadership?"

One tactic was to keep Sal on for several months during the transition. Another was to carry out The Café's style of treating employees the way they would want to be treated—an approach Johnson calls a "servant-leader mentality" he says they strive for at their other restaurants, and Kapfhammer more bluntly calls "giving a damn what's going on with them." Their plans include being in touch with the halfway houses from addiction recovery programs that have provided part of The Café's workforce.

Another tactic was to promote Christy Strauss to general manager of The Café.

❧

Strauss seemed an unlikely leader when she came to The Café in 2014, but she brought Sal and Cindy her own lesson on overcoming a stigma.

She shouldn't have been allowed to work there, according to The Café's employee handbook, which reads that, except for earrings, "No other face piercings are acceptable and will not be tolerated."

Strauss wears her hair purple. Large deep red and black tattoos run down her chest, up her arms, and over her fingers. She wears a nose ring.

Sal concedes the handbook is "antiquated," and says hiring Strauss "was almost the flip of a light switch for me." The Café's move from the Antique Mall took the business to a trendier part of town "where if we truly wanted to compete, we needed to be more accepting of the culture."

Then, Cindy says, her daughter came home from college one day with a tattoo and a nose piercing. "That doesn't really define who you are, Mom."

Strauss moved to Louisville from South Carolina, needing a job after a divorce. She started as a hostess, then after about two months, Cindy needed a replacement for the baker of The Café's iconic cakes.

"I was bussing tables with her one day and she says to me, 'I kind of like to bake,'" says Cindy. "I blew it off. I thought, 'That's nice, but what you do in a restaurant is not like home baking. You've got to keep your consistency so you can do the same thing again and again. You have to have a creative side and a factory side.' Christy took on both of those and she expanded it."

Cindy taught Christy patience with cake batter, when to stir with a paddle, and when to stir with a whip.

"Sometimes she'd get a little kookie, like her Skittle cake; she'd be all over the place with candies and that's not really us. We're more southern, traditional comfort food, not kid cake," says Cindy. "She took me seriously and listened, she stuck to the recipe, and she was able to recreate what I did. I let her prove to me she could do it, then all of a sudden she was coming up with these creations. She's taken it to another level.

"She has that mentality of entrepreneurialism and being something bigger. She's looking at recipes on Pinterest and she's constantly Googling. 'Oh, look, I think I could do that.' She takes ownership like it's her own little business but still takes criticism or suggestions. She took it and made it better. She's not who I saw in the bakeshop at all. That's what can happen when you give somebody a chance."

When The Café sold, Sal and Cindy recommended Strauss to be the restaurant's general manager. Sal describes her as "level-headed. She sees things for what they are and doesn't overreact. She has an ability to take in the whole picture."

Johnson saw her as "somebody who can connect the future with the past in a meaningful way. She's got this calm, self-assured, collaborative leadership style that's not cocky and not brash. The first thing I saw was fearlessness. She's not afraid to say what she knows and what she doesn't know. She's not afraid to learn. She's not afraid to stick her neck out and say 'I'm not exactly sure what I'm supposed to do, but this is what I think feels right.'"

She impressed Kapfhammer when he asked her what she wanted to be. "She said, 'I want to run the place.'"

☙

Strauss came to The Café not knowing about its practices of hiring refugees and people in recovery. She just found it "homey, welcoming, and warm." She talks with a kind of wide-eyed wonder and a take-things-as-they-come delight about the personalities she would meet navigating the restaurant and learning how it worked. "The ladies that work in the kitchen are incredibly wonderful. Sometimes they're hard to understand, but you figure it out. Charades are very big here."

She recounts first finding out that several of her co-workers came from addiction treatment programs: "I had no idea, so when I first started working here I worked with this lovely head hostess and she was telling me the craziest stories about her life. I couldn't believe it. How are you alive? How is this true? She explained that a lot of the servers are from recovery and I thought that made sense because of how welcoming and accepting people were. They don't care what your background is, just where you are at the moment."

Strauss asked Cindy about filling in for The Café's cake maker because she remembers liking to bake at home, even though her only experience came from store-bought mixes and a Betty Crocker cookbook her mom gave her.

"It's very precise, the procedures you have to follow to get this really good product," she says. "It's really good tasting, it makes everybody happy. It smells so good it makes you in a better mood."

Strauss pretty quickly figured out what the cakes meant to the customers. She could see them sitting on the table at the front door and watch Myra White selling slices at the carryout station. She noticed the customers ordering their cake first, to make sure they got what they wanted before it ran out. It took a little longer for Strauss to understand what the cakes meant to The Café.

"I knew when you walk in that's the first thing you see, that display case of cakes. People would come to The Café just for the cake—they'd go to Myra and get their to-go cake," she says. "Another thing that Sal and Cindy really put into my head is they wanted to keep it pretty much the way they made it. These are Cindy's recipes. That strawberry cake is her grandmother's recipe. It's good, it's amazing, everybody loves it, so it was really important to me to keep it exactly how they want it because, why wouldn't you? They're great."

Strauss worked with Cindy and the cooks in the kitchen, picking up the baking techniques along with the deepening sense of how the cakes fit into the success of The Café, "which also made me nervous because, oh my God am I going to be able to do this? But I got constant encouragement from Sal and Cindy. Then, all of a sudden, I was making cakes by myself. It just happened."

The three signature cakes are strawberry, Italian cream, and Tuxedo. There's a fourth kind of cake that changes each day.

"The cake of the day was my outlet," says Strauss.

She tried a maple bacon cake she says was a hit. "I think bacon and chocolate just go together so well." She made a Pride cake that displayed bright rainbow colors. She made an Almond Joy cake, a cookies and cream cake, a pumpkin spice latte cake "just to do something different and keep it fun."

Strauss laughs when I remind her about Cindy's reaction to her Skittles cake. "Sometimes I would do something that wouldn't fit The Café," she says. "I try to keep it pretty modest because the people that come in here are pretty modest."

Her body art isn't modest. A flamboyant tattoo of a large geisha covers the top of her chest, but she says it's never been an employment issue, despite the piercing ban still in the employee handbook. "Everybody's getting pierced and tattooed. It's not so uncomfortable anymore." She talks about what they mean to her.

"They're kind of a road map of what I've done and what I've been through," she says. "Instead of writing a journal I went and got a tattoo. They're pretty, they're not so messy, and I'm not going to lose them like you could lose a journal."

She has a tattoo of a mechanical heart—"we're all recovering from something"—to which she added a timepiece for her son, "because he's my timeless love."

Strauss puts her hands together, palms down on the table. Two tattooed letters on each finger spell out

STAY TRUE
LAME NERD

until she pulls her hands apart so they now separately read

STAY
LAME

TRUE
NERD

and she explains, "After I moved here it took me forever to get me to know me after my divorce," says Strauss. "I'm trying to stay true and I'm totally a lame nerd. I enjoy my nerdy things, my horror movies, my baking shows, my comic books—I like graphic novels. I'm trying to keep me, but I'm still trying to progress. That's what I love about Sal and Cindy. They're letting me be me while I progress in life."

Sal and Cindy brought a lifetime of hard knocks to creating a legacy that changed lives. The new owners Kapfhammer and Johnson understand that heritage, and they talk about growing The Café as a business while still keeping the culture that made it a success. If maintaining the character of The Café while adding evenings, Sundays, and alcohol sounds like a difficult dilemma, Strauss doesn't see that as a conflict at all.

"I never saw myself in a position like this but I've kind of already transitioned into it. I'm already communicating with everybody. I do a lot more office work, which is weird. I don't mind hearing about people's problems. I like working my way through a problem, not just in cakes but servers or bussers, if people need to just vent or help with a translation, or ask, 'Can you help me with insurance?'"

When people think about The Café, says Strauss, she wants them to think about "Cindy and Sal. This is theirs. They started it and I want it to be exactly how they envisioned it, how they got it going and kept it going. It's worked. Why would you want to change it? It works."

But The Café would change. It would open on Sunday. It would serve alcohol. It would serve dinner. For Strauss, that's not a contradiction, just the next step in an American Dream.

"I am really, really stoked about where The Café's going right now. When we move across the street we'll be opening for dinners. Our catering is going to expand. The baking area's going to expand. Everything's going to get better or bigger, but everything's going to be the same. The lovely ladies in the kitchen are still going to be making our breakfasts and our chicken salads. Everybody's going to get their slice of cake. It will just be busier. It will still be Tonya in the dining room and Karima and Shawn in the kitchen. Myra knows everybody that comes in here. She's still going to ask you how your grandbabies are and when are you getting married and all that fun stuff. It's still going to be us. It's just going to be us seven days a week."

❧

Looking ahead to their new lives, Sal and Cindy planned those things people plan for retirement—spending time with grandchildren, taking care of Cindy's parents. Cindy's looking forward to cooking for her family without the pressures of a restaurant kitchen. Sal will finally get the knee replacement surgery he's been putting off. Another thing they've been putting off since college is a trip to Europe. And they visited Clark where he's living and working in China.

They look back, proud of their legacy.

"I really feel validated," Says Sal. "We were able to create something that was a measurable success. It's pretty rare to be able to sell your restaurant with a concept intact. The rule of thumb is you usually need at least three restaurants for a businessperson to buy that concept and to continue that as a concept. For us to be able to do that is a major success and a validation that what we did was good."

Cindy says, "There is worth in it. It's viable.

"The industry is basically about using you up and spitting you out," she continues. "We got used up and spit out and we started realizing we didn't have to do that. If you pay attention, you can have good people; you can train people you never would've thought would bring you success. You can have a good outcome and not feel like you're the person you don't want to be. We did something good in the industry."

Sal has pulled his real estate license out of escrow and is renovating a duplex into an Airbnb, and, at a site in walking distance of where The Café used to operate in the former Antique Mall, he's planning some rental properties. The projects could be managed by daughter Lydia and son Alex.

"Our kids never wanted a career in the restaurant business," says Sal. "But real estate seems to interest them. We'll see how that develops."

They're looking forward to being a couple.

They talked about life after The Café, sitting in Day's Coffee, a shop where they used to hold their small staff meetings as they waited for the doors to open at the Antique Mall.

"From day one it was just me and Cindy, side by side, working," says Sal. "That grew into a business and she had her area of responsibility and I had mine. Yeah, we were there every day; we were a husband-and-wife mom-and-pop operation."

Cindy adds, "But we were operating a business."

Sal agrees. "Yeah, it wasn't like we were together."

Cindy continues, "We were always working and working and bringing it home."

Five months after Sal and Cindy signed the agreement selling The Café, they let their other family members celebrate Thanksgiving on their own, and flew, as a couple, to Florida for the holiday weekend with old college friends, visiting sites from their past.

The Sunday after Thanksgiving, Sal and Cindy drove around outside Miami, thinking about the local delicacy of stone crabs, unique to south Florida and the Caribbean. They're strictly regulated, they can only be harvested in the winter months, and then only one claw can be taken from each animal before they're returned to the water. As they wondered aloud to each other about the logistics of getting themselves to an immensely popular favorite restaurant for stone crabs, Cindy noticed a gourmet grocery store with seafood to go.

The store had stone crabs. They bought a claw cracker, mustard sauce, and a pair cocktail forks, an orzo salad, marinated green beans, mango—and papaya. Cindy says, "That's something you can't get in Louisville—really fresh, good papaya."

They took their picnic to a pavilion about a hundred feet from the ocean, where they could hear the waves and, if they stood or looked around the sea grape trees, watch the surfers. Sal and Cindy describe the scene, alternating phrases with each other.

Sal says, "There was a breeze; it was a beautiful, bright, sunny day, but we were under the pavilion."

"It wasn't hot; it wasn't cold," says Cindy.

"It was just beautiful," says Sal.

Cindy says, "You didn't need a sweater. You didn't feel like you were sweaty. It was like the perfect temperature. I was like, this is amazing; this is like…"

Sal finishes the sentence. "It was…like a date."

❧

Sal and Cindy once dreamed of running a restaurant named Scarborough Fair. The Simon and Garfunkel song is based on a ballad hundreds of years old, about two lovers asking each other to do unachievable tasks like sew a shirt without a seam or buy an acre of land between the sea and the sand. The song concludes that love doesn't require completing the tasks, but trying. As Sal and Cindy kept trying, they discarded things that didn't fit—like the original name they'd envisioned for their restaurant—and kept the much bigger things that would build the foundation of a dream that would grow, prosper, and endure.

Where Credit is Due

This book started with a group of people curious about the world. My fellow members of the Discovery Sunday school class at St. Paul United Methodist Church live to learn, examine, and even argue about faith from as many angles as possible. So it was only natural that one day we would hear from fellow church members Sal and Cindy, who talked about how faith informed their business model of seeing the human being beyond the employee. During their presentation my mind recalled an opinion I'd developed during years as a trade association manager and armchair social critic: "People are wrong when they say doing the right thing can be good business. Doing the right thing *is* good business." Sal and Cindy were living proof that doing the right thing is good business.

For the next few weeks I wrestled with what to do about the story Sal and Cindy told that Sunday morning. During my career in writing, editing, and periodical publishing, people would ask whether I was ever going to write a book. I'd quickly reply, "No. Too hard."

So when I finally gave in and realized Sal and Cindy's story was too compelling to resist telling, I knew I needed help.

One of the first things I needed were knowledgeable encouragers—longtime colleagues who knew about writing, books, and life in general. Those would be Nancy Grant, Jeff Almen, and Mike O'Brien.

They told me I could do it, how I could do it, and, in one case, that I had to do it—they had a relative struggling with addiction.

The basis of this book is more than eighty interviews, plus follow-up calls, with thirty people who gave me something much more valuable than their time: their trust. I'm still not sure why they showed such patience and faith with my sometimes deeply personal and other times darn fool questions. I thank them all that they did.

I got brilliant help from people who navigated and fact-checked my way through cultures foreign to me: Larey Correll with his experience working with Kentucky Refugee Ministries; Cindy Lamb and Gary Luhr for lending their sense of Louisville tradition to a non-native like me; Peggy Heimerdinger for trying to figure out what category a bookstore would put this book in, and for directing me to the helpful help desk at the Louisville Free Public Library; Margie Garcia and son Will Garcia for insights from people who knew the Rubino family well; and retired Col. Jim Wesslund—yes, my brother—for his knowledge of Air Force history and traditions.

So many people never mentioned in the limited space in this book made this story possible—all the employees of The Café, and all the members of Sal and Cindy's families. Special hero status goes to everyone remaking their lives and the staffs at Kentucky Refugee Ministries, The Healing Place, Volunteers of America, and Priscilla's Place.

I got good help finding my way through today's publicity and social media world from Lauren Hendricks at a+h marketing and Jen Carver and Ali Hawthorne at M2-Maximum Media.

Thank you to the test readers of the early draft manuscript to answer the scary question, "Did this book hit, or miss, the mark?"—Parker Bowling, Garrison Cox, Bob Gibson, Nancy Grant, Nan and Mark Tate, Amanda Thomas, Emma Wesslund. Thank you to recipe testers Nan and Karen Tate.

I want to recognize Wikipedia as essential to my research. I agree with the warning that authoritative writing should not rely on Wikipedia, but not using it as a starting point, supplement, and confirmation would be ignoring a powerful resource. Wikipedia is one of the great benefits of living in the Internet age—when it asks for contributions, give.

Two essentials to finishing this book and telling the world about it once I had finished writing are my editor, Lori Brown at Grammarwitch LLC, and Antoinette Kuritz with STRATEGIES Literary Development. They went far beyond those roles with questions like, "What do you want to be doing in two years?" and "Can you write an additional chapter?" and holding my hand on those dark days when I was sure this book would prove a disastrous waste of two years of my life.

I appreciate the countless other kindnesses from people like Bruce Maples, who so willingly allowed me an extended sabbatical from my advocacy writing for his *Forward Kentucky* progressive Web site; and from Mark Tate who bought me that beer at the Sunset Grille on North Carolina's Outer Banks after watching me spend one of my days at the beach transcribing an interview.

No one kept me going like family, wife and daughter, with their kindness, intelligence on matters large and small, knowing when to stay out of the way, and also willing to use their unique positions to tell me when I had a stupid idea. Finally, many of the opening chapter paragraphs sprang from the creative power of long morning walks through the neighborhood with our beagle, Bentley, whose manic sniffing and leash-tugging show he always believes something good is about to happen.

About the Author

Paul Wesslund grew up in St. Paul, Minnesota, where he went to Macalester College. He worked four years as a reporter and copyeditor at daily newspapers in North Dakota, then moved to Washington, DC, to work at the National Rural Electric Cooperative Association as an energy writer and managing communications and community involvement programs. He worked the next twenty years as editor of *Kentucky Living* magazine and vice president for communications for the Kentucky Association of Electric Cooperatives in Louisville, before retiring to do freelance writing and communications consulting. He's married to the former Debbie Thomas of Seminole, Oklahoma. They live in Louisville, Kentucky, and have a daughter, Emma, who works in theater in Washington, DC. When Paul's not writing, he's likely attending a concert or curating his collection of music that includes jazz, classical, alternative and classic rock, country, electronic, African Soukous, and especially the blues.